Rabbits
Don't Wear
Diamonds

Bernice & Bernie Christenson

By B&B Christenson

Copyright 494227
Copyright © 10/2001 by B & B Christenson

All rights reserved. No part of this book may be reproduced in any form without the written permission of the authors.

Canadian Cataloguing in Publication Data
    Christenson Bernie, 1925-
    Rabbits Don't wear Diamonds

Includes index.
ISBN0-9687515-1-2

    1.Pioneers-- Canada, Western –Anecdotes.
2.Pioneers –West (U.S.)–Anecdotes. 3 Frontier and pioneer life–Canada, Western –Anecdotes. 4.Frontier and pioneer life–West (U.S.)–Anecdotes.
I. Christenson, B. (Berniece), 1927- II. Title.

FC3237.C495 2001   971.2'02   C2001-903344-3
F1060.C495 2001

Author   Bernie Christenson

Illustrator   Berniece Christenson

Printed and Bound in Canada in 2001 by
        Friesens Printers
        Altona, Manitoba

Acknowledgments

My Wife, Berniece, has spent hours advising, encouraging, checking and correcting. Without her help this would be nothing but a dusty old manuscript in a box in the attic. Then, too, her illustrations are the icing on the cake. I am taken by her sketch of Ben Talbot and his buddies riding back to the chuck wagon (page 39). I can hear the soft sound made by the saddle leather, and smell the early morning dew on the sage.

To Jim Lyding a big Thank You for going back to his English class for his red pen, and correcting two hundred and eighty-seven pages of essays.

For checking and direction, I thank my sister, Joann Woods.

To family members, Margaret, Jim and Glen, your help meant a great deal.

Rhonda Christenson was again the editor. Many Thanks.

To every person (living, or those that have gone to the Great Beyond) that have provided the base for each story, I am indebted.

The Author

Bernie Christenson grew up in the Hallonquist area of southern Saskatchewan. As a boy he took every opportunity to be around horses, this shows up in many of his stories. After high school he apprenticed in Auto Body mechanics. This become part of his life, along with farming, and livestock.

Home has been Hallonquist, Regina, Lethbridge, Rush Lake, Leoville, and in retirement, Vanguard.

The Illustrator

Berniece Doll was raised on a farm at Hodgeville in Southern Saskatchewan and attended a rural country school. She worked in banking before marrying the author in 1951. For many years she was kept busy raising a family of 5 children. Art has been part of her life since her school days. Later, studying and teaching this subject filled many rewarding hours. With family gone, Berniece went to work at the Leoville Hospital as the Administrator. On retirement and free time available, she returned to enjoy painting and sketching.

Dear Reader:

We have made this book for you. If you could come over to our place and put your horse in the barn, we would have a good visit.

It would be no trouble to put another lump of coal in the heater, and we would set the coffee pot on the top to keep it warm.

We could sip our coffee, and enjoy the warmth from the heater, telling stories, on into the night. It would help us to forget about our isolation.

As that is not possible, take this book ,and if there are others around, share the memories that are tucked in between the covers.

      Sincerely,
      Bernie C.

Table of Contents

Grandad's Barn 1
Big Bang 4
Sale Goods 7
Buggy Wheels 10
Go West 13
His Horse 16
Log Drive on The Carrot 18
The Cow Is Out Again 21
Fast Horse 23
Money 26
Music Music Music 28
A New Life 30
Church & Fire 33
Bob's Ride 35
Differences of Opinion 38
Branded 40
New Rope 42
Quilting Bee 44
Clearing Land 1930 46
Village Band 49
Pigeon 51
Yu Fix Muy Truck? 54
Sheep and More Sheep 57
Some Change 61
In The New Land 64
Bush Pilot 69
Alfred Taylor 72
All Neighbours 74
Bilingual 76

Wheat	78
Black Diamond	83
Sandy Land	86
American Hunters	90
Just Wait	92
Harvest Time	94
Common Sense	97
Cut Down	99
Diphtheria	101
Chicken Today, Feathers Tomorrow	103
Never Say Die	106
The New Nash Car	110
Because Of A Nail	113
Cowboy Electrical	117
Nitro Jerry	120
Mr. Graham	125
Free Help	129
Uncle Chet	131
Horse Sale	133
Hunting	135
Watching the Frogs Spit	137
Mother Tongue	138
Simply Beautiful	140
Mr. Starblanket	143
I Killed Knute's Weathervane	148
Dexter	150
Bachelor	154
Apple Pie	157
Changing Times	160
Feeding The Multitude	162
Cinders	164

The Broom Truck	167
Law at Work	170
The Electric Rabbit	172
Just Color	174
Bert's Car	176
The Sock Smuggler	180
Courage	183
Birding	186
Smart Girl	188
Bad Boys	190
A Holiday	192
Team Work	198
No Accident Just a Mishap	200
Trail Blazers	202
Step on the Gas, Rabbit	205
The Last Kernel	207
Rabbit got Home Free	209
The Rescue Crew	211
Down the Creek	214
The New Job	216
Some Luck	220
The Red Truck	223
Too Little To Smoke	228
No Got	230
Harry Bill	237
Black Spark	240
Bits from Here and There	242
Lonesome Dog	244
First Request	246
Youth	249
Twister	252
Dirty Dishes	256

That Rabbit	261
Hit the Jackpot	263
Tornado	265
More Jackpot	268
Another Jackpot	270
Bedtime Story	271
The Bird Bath	274
My First Sheep	276
Love a Horse	279
The Ford Coupe	283
Rabbits Don't Wear Diamonds	285

Grandad's Barn

Today's farm boys have such a mountain of things to learn. There are planetary gears in tractors, micro chips in the controls of many implements, and herbicides, pesticides, fertilizers, and the list goes on and on.

When I was a toddler there were none of those things to be found on a farm. We put seed in the ground and if it rained the crop would grow. When the grass turned green, the cows and horses ate it and got fat. It was so simple but, boy oh boy, was it exciting.

Grandad's barn was divided into three parts, cows at the north side, horses in the bigger center section and sheep at the south side. As a four year old I was allowed to walk carefully down the center of the horse barn. Oh it was exciting! If the east doors were open, I could see out in the corral. Uncle David or Reinhart would be putting new shoes on a road team. Those were horses that would be driven on the road to haul the grain wagons to town. If I stayed well back and did not raise Cain, I could watch. If I made noise to bother a horse or an uncle, I would be banished faster than a deposed Sultan.

Dolly and Charm were a team of horses that were in their stall near the east end of the barn. Some times Grandpa would lead Charm to the door and I could take her to the water trough. When she had her drink, I would lead her back to the barn. That job gave me a glowing look at my ability.

Charm was a white horse. Dolly was a blue roan. One day Uncle David brought Dolly to the door. He handed me the halter rope then grabbed me under the arms and in a wink I was riding Dolly to the water trough. Life just could not get any better, until Dolly finished her drink and walked over a few yards and nibbled grass. Holly cats, terror set in. This was not in the plan at all.

"Help."

"Don't call for help. Ride her back here," Uncle David made sure that I understood that I would not be pampered. "Pull on the halter shank and kick her with your heels. Make her go."

The stress was smothering me. I did not think of where we might go, but we went. Faithful Dolly turned and went back to the barn. At the time I was too shook up psychologically to take pride in my accomplishment.

Minutes later I bragged to Grandpa, "I rode Dolly to the well and back to the barn."

He was a good friend, "That was nice but when you are four years old you should not ride too far."

(Three years later I rode Dolly to the Nybo school, where I did not learn too much).

I was still a pre-schooler when I lay on the hay in the loft and looked through the feed hole in the loft floor. I watched Uncle Sidney light up the singger. The tool was shaped like the candy scoop at the store only it had a tank full of kerosine and when it was lit there was a blue flame along the front edge. It was used like a curry comb, only it was after lice. Uncle Sidney said that when a louse hit the singger there would be a pop, and the louse would explode. The bull had to stay in all winter long and he would get lousy. I was too far away to hear the lice pop, but Uncle Sidney said that they did. My, but that was exciting. It was even more exciting one day when I was peeking from the hay loft .The hired man was going to feed the sheep. The ram charged. Engvold got out of the way but the feed pail did not. The pail got a great big dent in the side of it. It was fun to be in Grandads barn.

That was in Canada. In North Dakota Grandpa had a bigger barn when they lived there. There they cut hay on public land near the Sheyennen River. It was hauled home and put in the loft with hay slings. I did not learn much about that barn, except that Uncle Sidney hurt a leg and had to go to the doctors at Rochester, Minnesota.

The barn Grandpa had in Montana was quite small. He and Grandma were young then. It would hold four cows and a couple of saddle horses. It was empty one summer day. A small band of Indians stopped for bread and jam. They had their treat and rode away, but one pony was left.

Grandma went to the barn to see why one pony was still there. In the barn there was a pole tied to the manger and the other end swung on a rope from the ceiling. This was to separate two cows. The Indian lady had spread clean leather under the pole and knelt and leaned on the pole and had her baby. She was just cleaning the little guy up with moss, when Grandma came to the door. The mother without a smile but still friendly showed Grandma the face of the little tyke. She put the papoose in her back pack and got on her horse and rode away to join the band.

There were so many wonderful things that happened in Grandad's barns. If I knew all of them, I could write a book.

Big Bang

When I was seventeen years old and struggling through a grade of high school, one of my good friends was Mark Vanwarmer. He was only seventy then.

Mr. Vanwarmer had been in the Vanguard area in 1905. That was when the Turkey Track ranch had a winter bull camp at the bend in the creek just south of town.

Mark helped to foster my love for local history. That did cut into algebra and the rest of the math family. But that was a good thing, because with calculator and computer, I don't use much algebra these days.

It was in 1906 that I guess he and Grandma Vanwarmer were living on the farm where they spent so many years. Nearly forty years later they would go for winter retirement in Vanguard, but when spring came they were back to the farm just as busy as ever.

There came a day when meat was no longer on the menu in the summer of 1907. Mark hitched a horse to the buggy and drove about fifteen miles east. He was hunting for a deer. There is a deep coulee that starts as two small steep sided ravines that join, and are the making of the deep coulee. At the junction of the branches there is a small cone shaped hill. It is an odd place for a little hill in the bottom of the coulee.

When I saw that dome it had a wooden cross at the top. That was the final resting place of a pioneer couple. Mark had been there before the wooden cross was put up.

He unhitched the horse and tied it to the back of the buggy. It could rest there while Mark was deer hunting. He made his way down the steep side of the coulee and worked west against the breeze. Nearing the cone-shaped hill he spotted a deer. It was resting in the shade on the north side of the hill. Mark dropped down on one knee and raised his Winchester rifle. Taking aim he fired and the deer dropped over. He stood up and so did the deer. It looked around to see what was going on. It had never seen a hunter in its lifetime.

'Well, what the heck is wrong with my shooting?' He shot again and ran to the deer. He had two deer on the ground. The first one was a young buck, the second was an enormous big buck. That was where the problem began. The small animal he could dress out and carry it up the hill to the buggy. The other one was too large for that so he would have to bring the buggy to the deer. The day was well spent. Where was there a place to get the buggy into the bottom of the coulee? A few miles of searching and he drove to the deer. The smaller one he tied on the back and the larger one he struggled to get across the front of the buggy. Mark had to walk beside the buggy and drive the horse from there until they gained the level land beyond the coulee.

He sat with his feet on the deer carcass until after midnight when he got home.

The next day was taken with preserving Venison. In 1907 this pioneer couple did not have enough sealers to accommodate two deer. Every known method of keeping meat was put to use. Not a scrap was wasted.

Things got better as the years went by. New linoleum for some of the floors, embossed metal ceiling tile in the living room and in 1938 a new battery operated radio.

It was in their retirement years that they told me of this episode. They both had tears of laughter in their eyes when the story was finished.

It was a cold day when Mark took his .22 caliber rifle and went rabbit hunting. With his tobacco pouch in his vest pocket and his sheepskin coat on he went looking for a rabbit or two. He put a box of .22 shells in his vest pocket. There they would not be so cold and hard on the fingers when he had to reload his gun. He had a long walk and brought home three rabbits. They were food for the dog and cats. He took off his winter clothes and found that during the hunt his tobacco pouch had opened in his pocket and the shell box was rather squashed.

Work for the day was done, and the evening meal was finished. Mark was completely relaxed, engrossed by what the man in the radio was saying. Taking his long straight stemmed pipe from the smoker stand beside the radio, he reached the pipe into his vest pocket and packed it with the tobacco spilled from the pouch. He soon had a bed of red coals in the pipe bowl. He did not know that he also had a .22 long rifle shell in his pipe. He sat with his right ankle resting on his left knee. Between puffs on the pipe he would hold his index finger curled over the pipe stem and resting that hand on his high bent knee.

BANG, Mother came rushing from the kitchen, her dishpan was neglected.

"Ding Blast It," was Mark's response as he looked at the short piece of pipe stem still in his hand.

"Yes, Blast It. With what used to be your pipe you have blasted my new ceiling tile," observed Mother Vanwarmer as she looked very disapproving at the little hole in the ceiling.

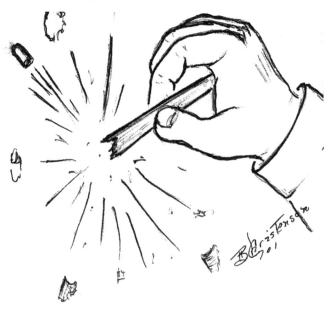

Sale Goods

People set out to claim western homestead land. Their plan was to save enough money from some poor paying job to get established on a farm of their own. Some men saved and scrimped until they were no longer young. Over the years, the dream of free land was kept alive. A young guy could start out from the U.S. Eastern sea board, and work his way west to Kansas. There would be no land left to homestead there, so on to Nebraska. Then north, the same situation was found in South Dakota, North Dakota, and Montana. At the turn of the last century, the only hope left was to go to Canada.

This poor pilgrim had made his way to Big Sandy, Montana. He worked at odd jobs through the winter months. The snow melted, and our man bought a team of horses and a light wagon. With the small amount of money he had, you can be sure that he did not buy the greatest trail outfit. The wagon at one time may have hauled watermelon, a way down south. It was small and weather beaten. The harness was adequate and with a big needle and waxed thread, and some lace leather, it could be repaired and it would do until the good times would come. The black mare, Lucy, was a prize. Her mate, Soda, was not much of an animal. At Haver, Montana, Soda seemed to be sick. When our traveler reached Turner, Soda was nearly dead. Our Pilgrim made a horse trade that he could barely afford. He swapped Soda and a few dollars for Tom, a sorrel gelding that was a much closer match for Lucy. Now, Pilgrim had a good young well matched team of horses.

The horse trader was rather hesitant about parting with Tom. That was the impression that he gave Pilgrim. In truth there was no halter shank, or fence that could keep Tom from coming home. At the right time he could be sold again. Oh, he was a money maker for his owner.

Our friend was on his way to Swift Current, Canada. Very few people south of the 49th parallel bothered to try to pronounce Saskatchewan. It did not matter, it was in Canada anyway.

Things went along good until Tom got home sick. He felt that he was getting too far from the grassy plains of northern Montana. One night he started on his way home. The Pilgrim climbed on Lucy, riding bareback, he went after Tom. That little side trip took up most of that day. Tom tried it again the next day. Luck was with the Pilgrim. A few miles back, along the road to Montana, some kids came out and told how their dad had caught the wandering horse and put it in the barn. They were supposed to watch for a man riding a black horse and tell him where his other horse was. Pilgrim rewarded each with a five-cent piece. They felt rich. He felt pleased.

You may think that this guy had a rabbit's foot in his pocket. That night he was able to keep his team in a farmer's sod barn. Tom was still there in the morning. The Pilgrim told his host about Tom and the problem he was causing. Mr. Bouraseu had the answer.

"You with the rasp file the hoof of your black horse. You keep the file dust and feed them to the orange horse. When they eat side by side for some tree day, the orange horse tink he the colt of the black horse," the short solid Frenchman advised.

"What will happen if the horse gets away again?" the Pilgrim asked.

"From de Swift Current you are tree long day drive. You need de rasp to cut de hoof. You need de chain to tie de orange horse to de wagon axel. Eef he pul sideways de wagon to Montana he ees easy to track."

Our Pilgrim saw the wisdom of this, but it also raised a problem. "I have no rasp and I have no chain."

"I sell to you dem tings. I, me got two rasp and tree chain."

Now our neighbor along the road, that had an accent, had crossed the prairie from the Red River settlement. He too had come west for a better life, but money was scarce around his place, too.

"No cost for you to stay. For de rasp one dollar, for de chain tree dollar. You put on orange horse neck, and tie with leather string, de odder end to wagon and your horse der in morning. Four dollar make you good horse."

The Frenchman, maybe it was he that they named the Frenchman River after, was pleased to regain four dollars.

The Pilgrim that fed hoof filings to his new horse was pleased to find that Tom would not leave Lucy's side in fair weather or foul.

The fella in Montana had sold Tom for the last time.

Buggy Wheels

School homework was not the greatest evening entertainment in my young life. At the dining- room table with my math books spread in the light from the kerosine lamp, I was faced with a whole page of questions to answer about circumference, diameter and radius.

"Mom, why are the rear wheels on a buggy bigger than the front ones," I pondered?

Mother gave it some thought, "Well, I can't give you a scientific answer, but I think it is to make it easer for the buggy to turn corners. If the front wheels were as big as the big rear wheels, they would rub on the side of the buggy when you turned a sharp corner."

She was sitting in her straight back rocking chair knitting mitts for Joann or myself. Folding her hands in her lap with the needles and yarn she remembered:

It was a few years after Pa had built the new house. I suppose that it was your Aunt Emma that got the Halloween party started. There were young people from around the neighborhood at our house that night. We played all sorts of parlor games. One was rather wild. Ellen Ekdahl was the youngest girl there. The chairs in the living room were in a circle with a space at the door. Beside the door we had pinned up a drawing of a donkey without a tail. Ellen was blindfolded with a dish towel and handed the donkey's tail with a big pin in it. Carl Nelson, a young bachelor, was asked to stand up with his back to the circle. They told him that he would be the next one to put the tail on the donkey.

Someone turned the blindfolded Ellen around a few times to get her confused, and then pointed her to Carl Nelson.

"Carl, you are supposed to bend forward, if you are going to be next." Such advice.

"More to the right, Ellen," that was more crazy advice.

"Put the tail on the donkey and push hard."

When Ellen heard that she took a quick stab with the tail and pin. Her arm just brushed Carl's hip. Annie sitting beside Carl's chair grabbed the girl to keep her from falling and hurting herself. Carl straightened up and joined in the laugh. He saw how he had been set up to get a pin in the rear.

The party went on for a while. Then we had sandwiches, cake and coffee. It was not long after that everyone went home.

Pa was going to blow out the light and go to bed when he heard a buggy stop. There was loud laughing, much swearing and some singing. It was the Ostrem brothers and they were tipsy. Pa tied their horse to the gate post and got them in the house and gave them cup after cup of leftover coffee. That sobered them up a bit so they took off for home. They lived in a dugout in the creek bank south of where Hallonquist is now. They were about four miles from home.

Pa left the light in the kitchen and went to bed. It was a while later that the same noise woke him up. This time it was loud talk and a lot of swearing. It was the Ostrem brothers still drunk.

"Good evening, Shir we shaw your light and thought that you could tell us how to go home. We had a sip of wine over to Campbell's, and we got lost in the coulees on our way home." The brothers were both talking at the same time.

Pa looked at the buggy and knew why they were lost. There were both rear wheels on one side of the buggy and the front wheels on the other side. Someone had switched the wheels while the Ostrems were having coffee. And, George and Sidney had come in and gone to bed just before the Ostrems were leaving.

Pa said ,"You guys come with me." He led them upstairs.

"Boys! Get out of bed. You guys can sleep on the floor." None of us ever argued with Pa.

George and Sidney slept on the floor while the drunken Ostrems slept in their bed.

Mom finished with, "That is all I know about buggy wheels."

Uncle Sidney told me a similar story. "Ostrem's drove into the yard after the Halloween party. They had been over at George Campbell's and got a snoot full of booze. Pa took them in the house for coffee. Some one switched their buggy wheels and they got over west in the field and drove in circles. The buggy was tilted to one side so they were sure they were lost in the coulees. One guy would drive the horse for a while, then the other guy would take over. He was lost, too."

"George and I switched their wheels back before Ostrems got up. They never knew what their trouble was."

Go West

It was a hundred years ago that Bob Burns was a teenager growing up in Ontario. From his earliest time he had heard Go West Young Man, Go West. Burns has to be a name for people of Scottish descent. Bob, the little Scotchman, had an Irish sound to his talk. By little I mean that he was less than five and a half feet but more than five feet tall. As a young man maybe he was taller, but age had possibly shrunk him some by the time I met him.

We were working on Norman's Plymouth in front of his garage.

Bob Burns Sr. strolled down the back lane. He was chewing something, and what ever it was, it was being treated like plug tobacco. Bob stood around and visited. The weather, the harvest and all the rest of the small talk drifted by, then he started remembering.

"Norman, me and your Dad done many things together in our young days. Wee Tom was thirteen that fall and I was eleven. We was sent out to clean up the buildings at the woods camp. We left home afore the sun was up. We carried our food for four days and walked seventeen miles to the camp."

Bob was such fun to listen to. One time someone said that he was murdering the King's English. With a smile Bob acknowledged, "Yes, I suppose the King is English."

They did not carry food for four days. It was to last them four days. And I should add that Mr. Tom Woods as I knew him was not wee.

One of the Wharton boys was driving his grandmother to town. Near the Woods farm the old car jumped out of the set of ruts and was stuck in the mud. Grandma sat in the back seat. Tom with his back to the car lifted the rear wheels back into the tracks.

Someone asked, "That would be a terrible heavy lift."

Tom replied, "Yes, Granny weighs over three hundred pounds." He did not want her to have to step out in the mud.

Yet to Bob Burns, his friend would always be the Wee Tom.

"We wuss supposed to clean up the cook house first. It was the afternoon what time we got there. Wee Tom told me to sweep the dust off of the table and benches. He made a big fire in the cook stove. I swept the floor and Wee Tom took a pan of water and soap and washed the table off. It got dark so we lit the lamp and had our supper."

"The building was made of logs and chinked with mud and moss. Wee Tom asked if I had seen a scissor. I said Aye and went and got it for him."

"Now come and hold the lamp and the dust pan."

"Wee Tom had me hold the light near the wall. Soon a garter snake stuck his head out to see what was going on. The Wee Tom took the scissors and sniped it's head off. We cleaned seventeen snakes out of the mud and moss chinking in the cook house. When Wee Tom got through with the scissors I had seventeen heads in the dust pan."

Bob shivered at the memory, " Twas a creepy job but I had a worse one on my first night in the Vanguard country."

"I had hitched a ride with a feller with a team and wagon. He told me that was as far as he would go. So I was supposed to walk over the hill and go three miles more and I would come to the house where I would stay until my brothers were located. When I got to the house, I found it had one door and one window on the east side. It was one room about so big. (He indicated by motion and ground markings that the house was perhaps sixteen feet square.) There was a letter with the fella's name on it so I was sure that it was the right house. I found something to eat and went to bed. I was tired so I went right to sleep. When it was pitch dark the mice in the chest of drawers woke me up. I got out of bed opened the door and tip toed over and listened to the mice. I very quietly slid the drawer out and set it outside. Then I went back to bed. I was just about to sleep when the mice got noisy. I got up and took another drawer outside. There were six drawers in that piece of furniture. It was near as high as I was. I had to get out of bed six times that night."

This shriveled up little Scotchman with the Irish accent wearing his winter coat on this sunny, but cool fall day started a pantomime.

On the bare ground of the back lane, Mr. Burns got woke up, got out of bed and carefully removed a drawer that was full of mice. It was oh so gentle and smooth an action to carry it twenty feet and set it down. Turning to Norman and I, he said, "You had to be so careful so the mice did not get scared and jump out again in the house."

His Horse

The problem started because he loved his horses.

Ole was born in Norway. When he was a young man he made his way to North Dakota. The so called free land was all taken in Dakota, but there was still plenty left in western Canada.

He came to Saskatchewan and got a homestead. He started with one quarter section of land and a team of horses. As the good life came his way, he got more horses. Among his outfit of horses, Jiggs was a favorite. Of course Ole still had an accent so his best horse was called Yiggs. He had horses but no wife or children. His horses and land were his complete life.

The years rolled by, and as he got older, Yiggs developed a bad front leg. A neighbor wanted to buy the horse, but Ole did not trust the fella to give the animal the care that it should have.

As time went on, even good loving care did not cure Jigg's leg. The next step was to give the horse its everlasting sleep. For this he called on a friend for help. This friend brought his rifle to use for the job. The poor horse that had so much pain that he could not even eat enough to keep from getting poorer and thinner, got shot in the head. There was an accident. Ole got shot in the leg, too. Ole's leg was finally amputated above the knee.

Sure the operation on Ole's leg saved his life but it was far from a success. The pains that shot through his body, from time to time from the stump of a leg were very near unbearable.

Willie and Chow had come from China to the prairie about the same time as Ole had come from the U.S. Their life work was to provide meals for hungry people that came to their café. These two men had the respect of the entire community. They held that place and that love of their fellow men for more than thirty years.

The horse was gone and the leg was gone, so there was nothing for Ole to do but close out the affairs of the farm, and go and live in a room above Willie and Chow's cafe.

The only pain killer Ole would use was whiskey. The part of his leg that remained gave him terrible pain at times. During the night if he was sober he would scream in his sleep, if he was able to sleep. If he was under the influence of alcohol he would moan very loudly during the night. For years this kept on. The sound of Ole's agony did not help Willie and Chow to get a solid night's sleep. Besides the moaning and screaming and swearing, Ole became not the cleanest house guest. With the confinement of the small room and no future it is no wonder that he became rather sloppy in mind and body.

The years were very trying for Willie and Chow.

When Ole finally went to find Yiggs in the great green pasture out beyond, there was peace and quiet for one Norwegian and two Chinese.

Log Drive on The Carrot

Shorty Abbott was a young man when he came to Saskatchewan from Wisconsin. He was not a giant of a man, in fact he may have been near the other end of the scale. I would not be the one to judge his size. When I met him, he was ninety-four years old, and in a hospital bed.

Shorty worked for a logging company. All winter long they piled logs on the ice of the Carrot River. The plan was to have a boom made up when the ice melted, and drive the logs to the sawmill miles downstream. At the mill they would chain enough logs together to make a barrier across the river. That would keep the log drive from going right on past the mill.

The only trouble with this plan was, the flood that spring, came before the boom was made up. It left logs hundreds of yards from the river channel. To correct this, the company sent out crews in boats. The men would get in the flood water and pull the logs back to the river.

The boats were made of planks, and it took a man on each side with an oar. The boat was too big for one man to handle both oars. Each crew consisted of a boss and six men. In the boat they had chains to put on the logs so all six men could grab on and pull. They had canthooks, crowbars and axes to use on the job.

Shorty said that they would be in the cold water most of the day. At the night camp they would dry their clothes the best they could at the camp fire. The first four days the boss was a prince of a guy. When they were so far down the river, that it would be very hard to get back to the main camp, the boss became a slave driver. All he did was sit in the boat and scream and swear directions to the fellows in the water. This went on for three days.

There was a big Indian on our crew. We were working near the south edge when the Indian guy said, ' I think this is where the old people used to come for Maple sap. You guys work slow but don't let the boss try to get the boat over here. I'll soon be back' He came back and said that the old trail to Hudson Bay Junction was close and we could be there in four hours. The crew all stood on firm ground in their wet clothes, and waved goodbye to the man screaming and swearing in the boat. They also said goodbye to the remainder of their wages. Four hours later they were seated in a café at the Junction.

The pork chop was good and the thought of the boss out there alone was even better. He would have to float down river 'til he came to another crew, but then he would not be boss. He would be out in the cold water pulling on a log chain.

Mr. Shorty Abbott worked at Big River for a time. He then was with the survey crew that staked out the sections of land. A long time later we were going to raise cattle on some of that land.

I asked him, "Shorty, do you remember what the land is like on section eighteen?"

"Which eighteen do you mean?"

"The one west of the Walter Woods homestead," I answered.

"There is a ridge of aspen along the north side, heavy spruce timber on the southeast and grass and willows in between. You will have to look for yourself. It has been over seventy years since I saw it," he replied.

What a memory! The land was just as Shorty said it was.

Shorty left his aches and pains behind, as one day he went to explore the Great Beyond.

Eph Mckellep was in his seventy's.

"When I was a kid, I met Shorty, and we stopped at this guy's place down in the Twin Bay area. Well, this fella was ready to tear his hair out. He had saved his land for the hay crop, and run his cattle out at Birch Lake. It was in late November and there was two feet of soft snow. A rain shower hit Birch Lake and cut across just west of Twin Bay. It left a one inch sheet of ice on the top of the snow. The farmer had made the trip out there on snow shoes to get his cows home. He had no luck at all.

He said that the thirty-five black Angus cows were in a tight little bunch in some spruce trees. If they walked in the ice covered snow, their legs would get cut and skinned. Shorty said to me that we should save the cows for this guy. We stayed there for the night. Shorty asked for all of the rags that they had around the place. In them years there were plenty of rags, but most people were wearing them.

After a very early breakfast, the lady had rounded up a fair size pile of old rags and cloth.

At the barn Shorty bandaged the legs of our horses. He wrapped them from the knees down. He explained that way the ice would not get into the rags when the horse put its foot down. He had gathered up a bunch of string off oat sheaves. We saddled up and went to Birch Lake. We rode single file and made a pretty narrow path. Every so often we would stop and Shorty would use some of the string to repair the leg bandages. We got to the cows and he told me to turn back, and ride slow. He stayed and came after the last cow. I did help to chase those cows one time and it was easier to get deer out of the bush than them black devils. That day it was different. I could look back and see, there were thirty- seven black cows on this one foot wide trail. One a few steps behind the one ahead. It sure did look good , the long string of black cows in the white snow. Shorty with his red coat was at the tail end. When those cows were in the corral, we got a lot of thanks and a heck of a good meal."

Eph ended his memory of Shorty by saying, "It did not matter how wild or mean a horse was. If Shorty got on a horse, he never got off until he was darn good and ready."

The Cow Is Out Again

It was at the north edge of the parkland, where there was a considerable amount of forest spread around.

There had been a rain during the night. Things were well soaked and the ground was muddy. Albert was out looking for trees that he could turn into fire wood. His search took him to where his land joined the neighbour's pasture. There were about forty cows standing there. Farther down the road was the farm owned by the local store keeper. This gentleman had a smart looking buggy team. He loved his horses and treated them that way. They would prance along, and it seemed that they would step on air and not touch the ground.

This morning it was different. The horses were stretched out in a dead run. The merchant sat in the buggy in the same position as a jockey. The buggy wheels were flinging mud.

That man was in a hurry.

Albert looked across the adjoining field and saw a police car slithering up the slippery road. What possessed him to do it he cannot explain. He opened the gate and shooed all the cows out on the road. They stood there as only dumb cows will. Albert waved the police to a stop. "Help me get these animals off the road. The darn cows are out again."

"We have no time for that. We have to go," was the lawman's answer.

"Did you ever try to run over a herd of cows when it was this muddy?"

"All right but we have to hurry." And the two officers became cow herders.

At last the cows were back where they had come from twenty minutes earlier. The road was messed up with cow tracks. The police car crept along in first gear for a long stretch before it gained speed. Albert and the cows gazed up the road wondering what it was all about.

The next time Albert was in the store, the gentleman with the fast horses said, "I finally figured it out. There were no cows out when I drove by. Yet the police were held up by cows on the road. So you opened the gate and put them out. That just gave me time to put away the many gallons of moonshine that were at the farm. I owe you a gallon, and I'll pay up this fall."

Albert told me, "I did not know that the storekeeper was a bootlegger, but we did know what to do with the jug of moonshine."

Fast Horse

Mom and Dad were married eight years before sickness took him away. In that time he had done every thing he could for her. The oak dining furniture we still use, even though it is eighty years old. The Old Homestead cook stove that weighed four hundred pounds, so they said while the crate was being removed. And then there was Billy.

I think that the items are listed in the order that they were given. That was at the time of their marriage.

Billy may have come later. He was a long legged sorrel colt. Mother just loved that horse. He grew to be a tall lanky animal with one white hind foot and a white star in his forehead.

I suppose that it was a hundred years ago that a great trotting horse named Dan Patch was able to trot, not gallop, just at a trotting gait and could go one mile in four minutes. Every one talked about Dan Patch.

When Billy was four years old, he was Mom's well mannered buggy horse. Grandpa's house was less than a mile and a half from our home if we cut across his pasture. Otherwise it was a half mile west, one mile south, a half mile west and a half a mile north to Grandpa's. He told me that he watched my Mom run her horse for a mile. Well, he did not see the very first of the run. Not until the dust on the road a half a mile away caught his attention did he watch.

Many years later Mom told how she tried out Billy. At the south end of the mile she had stopped across the intersection so when she crossed the mile mark Billy would be at full stride. She checked her watch and said Go.

Grandpa said that at first he thought that she was having a runaway. She was wearing a white dress and leaning forward in the buggy. If it was a runaway, she would have been leaning back and pulling on the driving lines. "That Sorrel horse sure did eat up the road," he claimed.

Mom said, "By my watch it took Billy about twenty-two seconds more than four minutes to go the mile, but it was up and down with gentle hills. How would Dan Patch have done on the track that Billy had to run on?"

Mother had used her heart shaped gold plated lapel watch that Dad had given her as an engagement gift, to time her horse. The watch kept time until the summer after Dad passed away, and that year the watch died, too.

Mom was left with three quarters of wind swept land, and my sister and I.

Dad had shown me the Big Dipper, and how the stars moved around the north star. When he died, it seems that a giant hand grabbed a bunch of sky and left a hole that the big dipper just misses on its circle around the pole star.

Childhood memories should all be happy. Some are not.

I suppose that I was finished with grade two. It was a hot day in July when Mom finally gave me permission to ride Billy down to play with Basil. It would be a little bit more than a mile to ride. There would be no boredom that day.

Mom put the bridle on and boosted me up on the tall horse. One of King Arthur's knights could not hold a candle to me. Here was me, up on this sorrel horse riding away. What a heady feeling that gave me.

In my travels there was a gate that was closed. I swung my leg over and by holding a handful of mane, I slid to the ground. The gate was easy to open and close, but to get back on Billy was not easy. When I got him beside the fence that I could climb up and crawl onto the horse, he would turn and look at me. That put his back so far away from me that I could not even dare to jump. The problem solved, I led him between a telephone pole and the fence, he could not swing his back end away from me. I got back on. I was riding again.

Uncle Albert was summer fallowing with his tractor, in the hills east of their home. He rode his horse to where he worked and tethered her out on the grass until time to ride home again.

He came to the yard from the east, I came from the west. We met, and there was Basil. I stayed on my horse and Basil was up in the saddle on his Dad's horse Delly. We rode south from the farmyard. It was a half a mile. At the east and west road we turned to go home again. The flys were bothering our horses. We were less than half way home when my cousin said, "Let's race."

Just like that our horses were on a dead run. It was a first for me, I had never been on a horse that was stretched out and running fast. We were getting closer, and riding neck and neck and not slowing down at all. Basil said, " Look at my Dad run."

There was Uncle Albert going as fast as he could to the barn. It was strange, boys run but big people can't run, at least you never see them do it.

The three way race ended at the barn door. Uncle faced us with his arms out wide. The horses stopped.

"You kids should not ride that fast. The barn door was open, and if your horses would have run into the barn, you both may have been killed."

During a life time, Basil and I have taken many rides together.

Money

Bill and I were sitting in a coffee shop, quite snug. The wind would drive a flurry of snow past the window every so often.

"I had taken a job for the winter at a sawmill in southern British Columbia. The work was a mix of mechanic and welder. I was supposed to be in camp all winter. There was to be no trekking out in the bush before daylight for me," Bill explained, "One morning I was one of the last ones in the cook shack. The foreman came and sat down with me."

"You better take on one more plate of pork and potatoes. I need help," he said, and sat looking mysterious.

When we went to his bunkhouse, he pulled a fur robe off a toboggan. There was a gray canvas bag tied on the sled. "We have to get this to town to-day."

Town was at least twenty miles if we followed the railroad. The snow was feather soft, but about knee deep. We figured that it would be about ten miles if we cut across. The snow would be less on the railroad, but then it would be twice as far. The short cut would take us across two ridges at the base of mountains and the town was in the valley beyond that last ridge. That was the trail we chose.

One guy would go in front to make a track, and the other one would pull the toboggan. The load was not that heavy, but it would get hard on your arms, so we changed often.

At the crest of the first mountain ridge, we had been ploughing thru knee deep snow for three hours, the foreman called for a rest. "Would you believe it, Bill. Yesterday when the train came by and the baggage man kicked out our grocery bag, I got this one instead. It is sealed up but the shipping order says that it is for the mine. There are nearly two hundred thousand dollars in that bag. You know that we are only three miles from the State of Washington. I lay awake all night. It was tempting. I could have been a long way south before they even missed this money. It would be a big job to exchange that much Canadian money for U.S. funds."

"This morning I knew that I could not live the rest of my life looking over my shoulder."

We figured that on the down hill runs we would both jump on the toboggan like when we were kids. In two feet of fresh snow it doesn't work that way. We walked and walked!

It was getting dark, we were up pretty high on the last ridge and could see the lights in town down there.

We were tired, and mighty hungry, up on the side of a mountain half starved and weary, with a couple of hundred thousand bucks.

"What darn good is money anyway?"

Music Music Music

It took six men to move the cast iron backed piano from the living room to the open air cathedral on the south side of the Nybo house. I called it a cathedral because the Lutherans were going to have their church service in the open air that Sunday afternoon in 1912. That was why the piano was brought outside.

Reverend Bjelde was there to conduct the church service. He was a large man with a no nonsense attitude.

Chairs and planks on boxes provided the seats. Against the white wall of the house the piano was centered, and the focal point to the congregation seated in rows, facing the house. The clergyman was to the right of the piano, and the choir was to the left. The men singing bass and tenor had their back to the wall. The alto and soprano ladies were in front of the men. The faint west breeze passed the choir, the pianist, and finally the Reverend Bjelde.

It may sound far fetched but these pioneers were not going to let an inconvenience like not having a wooden church with wooden pews, hinder their devotion. They still had their four voiced choir.

Every one was dressed in their so called Sunday Best. The senior couples were seated on chairs near the front. The wearers of fancy dresses and pressed suits found places on the plank benches. The bachelor homesteaders and cowboys that could only come with a white shirt and neck tie sat at the back of this cathedral.

The order of service was a prayer, a scripture reading, song by the choir, the sermon in which the craftiness of Satan was well pointed out , the choir again, and finally the closing prayer. Oh, there were hymns by the gathered worshipers thrown in here and there.

At the piano for every hymn and choir number was Mr. Hauser. He had newly arrived from Hamburg, Germany. Mr.

Hauser was a match for Reverend Bjelde. They were both large men.

Church was finished but the people sat while Mr. Hauser played classical music. He was a very skilled pianist. The Reverend sat on his chair a discreet distance from the piano. The beautiful musical notes wafted into the summer air.

A little no-account whirl wind passed by the piano, the pages of music were also up in the air.

"There goes my music blown to Hell," screamed Mr. Hauser.

The minister and the musician, two solemnly dressed gentlemen, were running after the whirl wind, waving their arms to grab any paper they could touch.

I suppose they both loved music and did not want the Devil to get it.

A New Life

It was in the spring, and the weather was warm, but it was too early to start farm work. I was helping John Solberg repair telephone lines. As they would say away down southwest, 'He had been up the stream and over the mountain.' Yes, John had been around many places and done many things.

He spent some time in South Carolina. He told of the black man that had been shot in the chest. The bullet glanced off his breast bone and left a white scar. With a deep voice and deep humor, he claimed that he was on his way to becoming a white man.

Digging a hole to reset a big cedar telephone pole took time and effort. The effort was mine, the time was John's. He had a bad heart condition, but was still the brains of the crew.

The timber country of Michigan was the first stop after leaving the south. A whisky soaked logger took pity on the twelve year old boy. He looked after the kid until they got to Spokane, Washington. The next thing John knew, he was alone on the street of a rip roaring city. A kind lady took him to a hotel where he was fed, and later employed. John saw much of the rough life of men in the logging industry. It was a man's hotel. A woman was seldom seen at the place. The guest rooms were the basis of the hotel but did not provide as much income as the dining room, and it was far below the bar room, as a money maker. His duty took him to every nook and cranny of the building. One carousing logger John told about. His name was Fir Bark Joe. It was a nick name, of course. He earned that name because he was as rough and coarse, as the bark on a fir tree. He was a large man; big, strong and muscular. He was also as hard headed as a fir stump. His life, was being out in the big timber for a month, working like a slave, cutting down the Douglas Fir trees.

Fir Bark was a good man on the crew for the time between paydays. When he got more than pennies in his pocket, he would go to town and become a roaring drunk.

One of John's duties was to clean the fish bowl in the hotel lobby every Sunday morning. This was a man's hotel and the fish bowl was man size. It was a big round cement tank that had an alligator swimming in it. This resident of the so called fish bowl was on its way to becoming a large reptile. When John worked at the hotel, the gator was about seven feet from snout to tail.

Benny, the hotel security guard and bouncer or peace keeper, would trick Ally, the alligator, with meat scraps from the kitchen. While the brute was after the meat, Benny would slip a leather belt under Ally's lower jaw and buckle it over the upper jaw, thus closing the big wide snout. Benny would lift Ally out of the tank and hold him upright with his wet belly to the sunshine. It was John's job to run ahead and open the doors for Benny and the alligator. The path was through the kitchen, out the back door to the back lane. At the other corner of the building was a stairway to the basement. There was a cedar plank water tank for Ally to rest in while John drained and scrubbed the fish bowl. If this was not done thoroughly once a week, Ally would smell as strong as some of the lumberjacks that spent their money in the bar room.

One cool Sunday morning, Benny had his arms around Ally, holding the gator just below his front legs. Its back was against the big man's chest, and the tip of its tail was dragging in the dirt of the back lane behind the hotel. Ally was on his way to the basement.

At the same time Fir Bark Joe was coming along the back ally, and where he was going, heaven only knew, because Fir Bark didn't know either. He was drunk. Benny did not have a chance to dodge around with the alligator in his arms, and Fir Bark staggered smack dab into Ally. He stuck his nose into the gator's wet and smelly hide.

The shock of that meeting was so great that Fir Bark Joe never took another drink. In fact, he got so good that he even doffed his hat to ladies on the street.

Church & Fire

Why the local church service was held at the Muri homestead, I don't know. There were other houses as big. On the other hand Mr. And Mrs. Muri were very devout people, and the minister had only a short mile and a half to walk to get to their place. As a bonus Mrs. Muri was a good cook.

The financial structure of a clergyman's income at that time was remarkable. First off, the young man who had just left the seminary had to find a group of people of his faith. Secondly, was there available homestead land? If there was land, Praise Be, they had a minister. There may have been a small bit of financial help from an old established congregation back east. With the money given for his support, there should have been directions for baking beans and boiling spaghetti.

The new minister had to depend on ploughing bees, to meet his homestead obligations. When he did have land ready to produce , again it was seeding bees, then harvesting bees. The neighbours had brought him here and the neighbours did the farming. He could not afford horses and machinery.

The base of the financial plan was for him to survive and when he grew old he could sell his land and retire.

It was a blazing hot Sunday. The minister was at Muri's for a Sunday beef steak dinner. Later wagons and buggies started to roll in. All of the chairs were set to face the corner of the room. Hemmed in the corner the minister had an apple box upended to put his hymn book and Bible on.

The overflow crowd stood in the kitchen.

The opening prayer, a hymn and then the sermon. There would be no maybe about it!

The sermon had just begun. It was soft to start with, but he would work slowly to the crescendo. Things were starting to warm up.

Some of the younger set, especially boys had not lived with saintly decorum. Boy! were they going to get Hell's Fire And

Brimstone to-day. He had seen the buffalo head on caps from the Calgary brewery. He would have rather faced a real buffalo than the one lying on the ground on a beer cap. Its sinful creepy roots could get into his flock!

Four of the Muri boys had snuck upstairs to their bedroom and changed to work clothes and down they came again. Other men left the kitchen. Soon the men seated on chairs got up and tip toed out.

In minutes the sound of water barrels in wagons, the bang of shovels thrown in, rattling wheels and galloping horses running to the west was heard.

It was not too far west either that the terrifying smoke cloud was rising. The male congregation had gone to fight a prairie fire.

The clergyman looked at the ladies seated there. Rather crestfallen he announced, "What's the use. Them that need it most are no longer here."

Bob's Ride

In July 1942 there had been a hail storm that raised cane with the rye crop on the Bessy place. This farm had just been bought by the Newall brothers, Bob and Fred. The Bessy place was maybe seven miles from the home farm and that was two miles north of Nitengale, Alberta. Beside the road to the rye field there was a tumbled down farm yard. The house was the most substantial building and it was a one room affair. Grey weatherbeaten boards turned away wind and rain. Two windows looked out to the south, and there was a door in between them.

When I moved the harvesting machinery past this place, there was a wisp of a man with white hair, in a chair, beside the door. He waved to me and I returned the courtesy. There was something different about his wave. His arm did not make circles in the air. It was a calm and dignified wave.

Every time I passed by there was that same motion. He slightly raised his fore arm, and with a short wrist movement and open palm, he did a Howdy that is still with me.

When we went by in the truck, it was always the same wave.

"Who is that old guy that sits in the sun all day long?" I asked Bob Newall.

The name he mentioned is forgotten, but it was Robert for a first name.

"He is eighty-four years old. Bob was a pioneer horse breeder. He brought his horses up from the States, long before there was any settlement in this area. He had his horses on Rosebud Creek. When the homesteaders arrived, there was no problem about horse power. Bob had well broke teams all over the place.

In 1919 he was well off. It was right at the top of the time of the horse business. There was not a man from one horizon to the other that did not owe Bob a favor or some money on a horse deal.

When the flu epidemic struck this district in the fall of 1919, a neighbour came to Bob's place late at night. The poor man was shook up. His wife had the flu and needed medicine from Calgary. It was a cold stormy night so Bob saddled his best traveling horse for the forty mile ride.

In the city he went to a livery barn where he was well known.

"Rub my horse down and look after him, he is near done in. Get my saddle on a good horse that I can ride home again. There may be a woman dying if I don't get the medicine to her quick." He took a street car up to Eighth Avenue and got the medicine.

With daylight and the wind at his back, Bob rode as fast as was reasonable for the livery horse. He went directly to the home of the flu patent. He handed over the package that he had carried in his vest pocket to keep it from freezing.

He turned towards home. He was just finished with eighty miles of riding. He was overtaken by a man with a team and sleigh.

"Bob, we have the flu at our place. Can you get us medicine from Calgary?"

"Yes, if you will get some one to cool down this horse, and look after my stock while I'm gone. Get one of the Johnson boys but get him here fast."

Bob was in the saddle when the neighbours came with help. "Look after the wet horse and get in the gray mare and have her ready for the road, just in case I need her."

The wind was still cold and the sun was down when he got back to Calgary.

At the barn, "Saddle me another horse and take care of this one. I'm in a hurry."

When he got back home, there was another ride for a prescription. He used the gray mare.

There was not a hint of daylight when Bob was back in Calgary at the barn. "My first horse must be rested. Saddle him up." He made another race across the snowy countryside.

Inside of his own house at last. The Johnson boy was sleepy .

"Bob, Henderson was over and they need medicine. I put your blazed face bay horse in for you."

"Good. Saddle him up while I grab a cup of coffee."

With the bay horse at the door Bob mounted up, and was on his fourth trip to Calgary.

Back at the livery barn, "Saddle the second horse that I rode in here. When this flu eases up, I will bring your horses back and settle up for mine."

"Well, Bob, this is your fourth trip to help people. I think that we will help in a small way. There will be no charge for saddle horse rent or feed," the barn owner promised.

At the drug store he asked, "Is it the same thing that I have taken every time."

"No, there has been a difference in most of them," the druggist answered.

"Could you fix me up a parcel of stuff in case someone else is sick when I get home. If this is to keep up, I won't have a saddle horse left at home, they will all be here in town."

"You must have been riding for over sixty hours. How can you stand it?" asked the man behind the counter.

"On a good horse you can sleep for a while and it sure shortens the trip. But it is very hard to eat while you are riding into a storm. But I got to go." Bob went.

The weather changed for the better in a few days. Bob rode a livery horse and led the rest back to Calgary.

Bob Newall finished telling this on our way home from the rye field that evening.

"That horse rancher was over sixty years old when he made the four none stop rides to Calgary."

"We will sure look out for the old cowboy if he needs help."

"He has outlasted every one of the people that he helped that time. Some moved away but most are gone for good, and there is not one of them to return the favor for old Bob."

Differences of Opinion

I did not know Mr. Talbot very well. He was leaning on the corral fence talking with my Uncle Sidney. I was too young to ask for explanations of what I did not understand.

Mr. Talbot's yarn went something like this.

There were eight of us in the crew. We had brought a herd of big steers to Topeka, Kansas. Our camp and chuck wagon were out of town about a mile. The boss said if we cleaned up, shaved and took a bath in the creek, we could go to town.

He also said, "No Guns."

It was nearly dark when we rode into Topeka. We tied up our horses and went for a drink.

It was strange, but at that time Topeka had black men in their police department. It seemed that they were half black, and half white. These guys also had differences of opinion.

We were just having a lot of fun when a bunch of black cops marched us off to jail. That did not bother us too much. We could sing in jail just as good as we could in the saloon or on the street.

We had been there an hour when a white cop came and asked us what we were in for.

We said, "For singing."

"I can understand that. It sounded bad, but that is not a great big crime," he said and turned us loose.

We were at a different saloon, just having a good time. Here come the black officers again. We were marched off to jail again. This time we asked on what charge were we being locked up for.

The answer was sharp and clear. "You are cowboys. That's why."

It did not take the white officers long to come and turn us loose.

The black guys found us right away. Two of them had pistols on them. There were a lot of hard feelings between Blacks and

Whites in those days. It wasn't so many years after the civil war and the freeing of the slaves. One cop made a motion toward his gun.

We explained that we left our guns in camp because we were such good shots we would be shooting flies off the walls in the saloons. The top man of this bunch kind of grinned. The other guy left his gun in his holster and we walked back to jail.

We hadn't sung more than part of a song, before the other cops came and let us go.

All night long the black cops cussed about the white cops, and visey versey. Between drinks we were marched off to jail.

It was daylight the last time the dark guys locked us up.

One of the white officers asked, "Are you guys getting tired of walking downtown from here? I'm getting tired of turning you loose. Why don't you get on your ponies and get out of town?"

We did.

Branded

The original homestead house was small and constructed in a rush with a low capital cost. It had two rooms, three windows and a door. It did not retain its door and windows once the big house was being built. They were removed and used in building the new house. Pa's shack then became the blacksmith shop. To my aunts and uncles, Grandma and Grandpa were Ma and Pa.

When Grandpa got back from the land titles office with the receipt for ten dollars that said the land was his, he laid out his building sights in his mind's eye. The first shack would be on the rise at the northwest of where the big house would be built. The barns and corral would be two hundred yards straight east of the main house.

There were two deep coulees, one coming from the south east, the other from the south west. They joined just north of the yard site.

The next five years made a marked improvement on the homestead. The big house was lived in and the old house had become the blacksmith shop. The barn was there with its high center section and a lean-to wing on each side.

One moonlit summer night at bed time, the blacksmith shop was brimming with activity. Grandpa went to the shop and the work stopped when he got his youngest son, eight year old David by the ear and led him off to bed.

At sunrise Grandma was building a fire in the cook stove so she could cook breakfast.Grandpa had his milking crew up and going. The sounds coming from the blacksmith shop meant that David was back at his unknown project. He had the forge blowing hot and the anvil was being used as well.

The gang with the milk pails were Grandpa, Emma, Olga, Sidney and George.

The cow herd was lying in the corner of the pasture on the flat ground at the edge of the coulee very close to the barn. To save time on a nice morning the milk cows were not put in the barn. They were all lying sleepily chewing their cud. A milker would nudge a cow to stand up, then position the milk stool, sit down and go to work. There was a blue roan steer that was about four years old lying at the edge of the herd close to the fence that divided the pasture from the yard.

The milk pails were somewhere between half and full when David came from the blacksmith shop . He was carrying an iron rod of some kind. It was his new branding iron with the foot high letter D. He was also coming so fast that you could practically see the soles of both shoes at the same time. The iron had been white hot when he left the shop. He ducked under the bottom wire of the fence and came up to Old Blue. He applied the red hot branding iron to the big steer's ribs. The burning hair caused a little cloud of smoke to rise, but when Blue woke up he was up in the air much faster than the cloud of smoke. His next move was to get somewhere else real fast. He charged through the standing milk cows. He did not moo gently. He went bellowing and snapping his tail. The milkers and their pails were upset and it spilled a lot of milk. The gentle old milk cows were somewhat agitated. So was Grandpa.

Old Blue did not wear that big D brand with much pride, but it was his for the rest of his days.

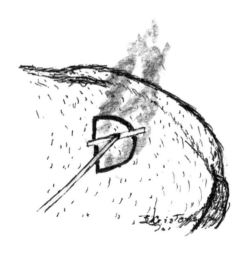

New Rope

Jack was an all right good guy, with maybe just the smallest touch of larceny in his heart. It was a long time ago that he told me this one. In fact, I was just a kid, and it was near the end for Jack.

Dad came home from town that morning. I went to put his team of horses away for him.

"Jack, here is a letter for you."

I shoved it in my hip pocket and put the team in the barn. After I had unharnessed the horses, I took out my letter.

June 26

Malta Mont Dear Jack:
                There is gona be a rodeo at Saco on July 4 You owe me ten bucks because that is what I had to pay to get you entered in the calf roping.
A friend has a hangout in town you can bunk with us. We'll see you before the fourth. You can pay me on the fifth.

                                        Yer Frend
                                        Slim Becket

Slim, was an old guy when I used to go down and ride in the fall roundups. He taught me all he could about roping. We were on the same crew for a few years.

I was a young guy, broke as usual. I went to Paw and asked for a few dollars so I could buy a new lariat rope, and some other things.

He asked, "Why?"

"So I can go to Saco, Montana to the rodeo."

"No need for that foolishness. We have work to do." Old John was tough and hard headed.

I rode into town and at the hardware store, I charged up thirty feet of cheap manila rope. It may have cost forty cents.

On the road home, I back braided the ends of my new rope. There was a big old Cottonwood tree out near the barn. I tied one end of the rope to it, and the other end to the wire stretcher, and it to the corner of the corral. I lit up the gasoline blow torch and burned off all of the lose manila fibers on the rope. The burning left little black dots all along the rope. Next I put a good coat of Ma's floor wax on the rope. Then I stretched it all I could. Every time I walked by the rope, I would give it a wax rub and more stretch.

I had a line backed buckskin gelding, and at daylight the next morning I was riding south. Pa wasn't even up yet. Well, Buck and I got to Saco the day before the rodeo.

The next day I won the roping. I got a few dollars and a bridle and saddle pad. I traded them to the fella that won the Batwing chaps.

A guy come up to me and said, "I know that a good rope will cost less than five bucks but there is a guy here that will pay ten dollars for your rope because you won first place with it."

I said, "Here is the rope, give me the ten."

That ten payed off Slim. I came home much better off than when I left. I wondered what the fella thought when he found out that his champion-ship rope turned into a dish rag.

Quilting Bee

It was just after noon on that January day when Mom and Aunt Ebba arrived at Grandma and Grandpa's farm. They were the first ones at the quilting bee. The quilting frames were set up in the living room. A sturdy kitchen chair was placed at each corner where the side boards crossed.

The frames were made out of eight foot long tongue and grooved fir paneling. These were the four inch wide boards that were put in the ceiling of most every house built in pioneer times. Grandpa had drilled small holes all along the length of these boards about six inches apart. A spike was slipped into the holes where the boards crossed. That way the frame was adjusted for the making of any sized quilt. They rested on the back of the chairs to make the quilt at working height.

The big square cardboard box that was filled with carded wool was brought down from upstairs. Grandma and Grandpa had shared the work with the hand carders. The wool had been washed then combed with the carders to make four by ten inch bats. These were stored in the big box for the quilting bee.

Alvin and Joann were the only grandchildren there so they were put down for a nap on Grandma's bed.

More of the family arrived and soon the quilt was surrounded by sewing ladies.

In the afternoon Uncle David came to the school and gathered the offspring of the quilters. We rode back to Grandpa's in the big sleigh. Come to think of it, Woodrow and I were the only ones that Uncle got at school. We had a cup of hot chocolate and went sleigh riding in the coulee north of the house. There were Woodrow and Basil and I, the school kids, and Joann and Irene the pre schoolers.

There was a bitter cold northwest wind, but in the shelter of the coulee we rode down that hill as often as we could lug our sleighs up again. There were little ice balls forming on every bit of wool clothing we wore. The girls had scarves over their faces. Their breath formed ice masks on the scarves.

We were having fun when Aunt Ebba with a coat thrown over her shoulders and just holding the lapels to keep it from blowing away, "Have you kids seen, Alvin?" Five No's came at once. She went back to the house.

By the time we got back to the house, Grandpa had his brown leather jacket on and had his mountain skis that he brought from Norway. He skied west to the edge of the coulee to look for Alvin. He returned, his eyes were tear filled from the wind. He gave the skis to a younger Scandinavian.

Anywhere you looked there were waves of snow banks they were the same shape as waves on a lake in a high wind. A little boy could be lying between any two of them.

Two of the uncles got on saddle horses and rode away. They would have a chance to look down between the snow drifts.

Every one was in the search. It had gone on for a full half hour. Alvin's hope for survival were getting dimmer by the minute. It was the general feeling that he had been left behind when the rest of us went sleigh riding, and he must have set out by himself to find us.

It was close to dark and hope was fading. 'Where could he be?'

Grandma just lit the lamp in the kitchen, and it disturbed Alvin. He crawled out of the over turned empty wool box where he had put in two hours of a restful nap.

"Where is everyone, and I am hungry." Then Alvin yawned.

Clearing Land 1930

Albert Laventure stood and watched the new Caterpillar Tractor clearing trees and bush to make farm land out of ground that was covered with Aspen and Willow trees.

'My she is a big one tractor that yellow one,' Albert mused as he watched.

The big yellow brute roared along knocking down the bigger trees.

The big yellow tractor's dozer blade was pushing over the willows when the front end of the machine dipped way down. The driver stopped and tried to back up. No luck, the tracks just piled up loose dirt at the front just behind the blade. The big Yellow Cat did not move.

Albert tied up the lines of his horses and stepped down from his wagon. He made his way across the tangled fallen tree trunks to where the tractor man stood with a look of utter disgust.

"Bonjour, Monsieur. You have trouble?" Albert greeted the cat driver.

The answer came with a snarl, "Big trouble." He then continued, "The closest machine big enough to pull me out would be in North Battleford. How far away from home am I?"

"It is about a hundred miles from here," Albert told him.

"I wish that I had passed up this job. By the time I get my bulldozer out of the mud hole, I will be broke. It will take a lot of money to get my cat out of here."

"Do you know if there are many wet mud holes in this field?"

"Yes, in the far corner there is a big one. Stay back from it with your tractor."

Further conversation revealed that the bush breaker lived in North Battleford.

"It is bad that you are stuck and it will be so expensive to get free of the mud. You should go home to your family and spend one day there. Then you come back and it may look better."

The Caterpillar man took that as good advice. He had a wagon to haul his fuel and grease that he pulled behind the cat from one job to the next. He had an old car tied behind the wagon.

Albert had done his farming with horses. This yellow monster was something entirely new to him, but his mind was sharp and working. Here was a situation just made for him - help for a fellow man, and a practical joke to boot.

As the cat man was undoing the tow bar that he pulled the car with, Albert asked, "The wheels with the tracks, are they free from the motor?"

The owner of the caterpillar had to straighten up and think of an answer to the question. "Oh, you mean is it out of gear. Yes, it is in neutral."

"You go home and have a rest, and don't spend money." Albert repeated his advice.

One man got in his car and was on his way to North Battleford. The other man got in his wagon and went home.

It was hard work, but to Monsieur Laventure it was between a joke and a challenge. He had returned with his big black horse skidding the stump puller. He had also brought a good supply of chains and lumberjack tools along. He cut four big logs off the downed trees. The first and longest log was placed in a three foot deep round hole he had dug. The other three were put into the ground in a line. The top of the first post was chained to the next one at ground level. The top of the second post was chained to the third post in the same way and it was tied to the forth. The stump puller was chained to the first post and its cable. Albert hooked onto the back end of the caterpillar down in the mud. The black horse was hitched to the long pole that extended from the drum of the stump puller. The horse walked in a circle around the stump puller. Each trip around wound up the cable and moved the cat a couple of inches. By sundown the black horse had made many, many trips around the circle. Now the yellow tractor was sitting out on dry ground. Albert removed the anchor posts that he had dug in, and smoothed out the traces of his work, and took his stump puller and tools home.

Albert just happened to be around when the caterpillar owner came back from his one day rest.

"There is my machine! It's out of the mud hole! How could that be!"

The caterpillar man was beside himself with joy. He could hardly believe his eyes.

"Who pulled it out?"

Albert stood there so innocent, and so casually said, "I did."

"But how could you?"

"Mon gros cheval noir."

Maybe the cat skinner could not speak French but he did catch on.

"Your big black horse? One horse?" There had to be a joker in the deck or one H of a big horse, but what the heck. There was the cat ready to work.

"How much do I owe you?"

Albert thought a second or two. The man had figured on a hundred dollars or more to get out of the mud. Then with a little bit of a mischievous smile, "Oh, will two dollars and twenty-five cents be all right with you?"

Village Band

When the Doll girls, Florence Siefert and Berniece Christenson, went to visit their cousin, Ann Major, the relationship took one more twist. The Doll girls, Florence and Berniece, were the children of Isidore Doll and Elizabeth Heembrock. Elizabeth Heembrock's brother Ed was Ann's father. So Ann was not a Doll girl by any stretch of the imagination.

Are you the reader slightly confused? Just wait.

Berniece had this beautiful old photo of the village band. It was taken sometime in the eighteen-nineties. The band members with their instruments held up so proud and shiny, looked so professional. Some of the more elegant mustaches must have been waxed. The three piece dress suits were much the same. The hats varied, but you would never find a fly speck on any one of them. The two rows of gentlemen standing so smartly, each with his piece of the brass band, were ready to make with the Oom-Pa-Pa.

Berniece had brought the picture along to show off her grandpa John Doll. He was the young man with the big horn at the left end of the back row. Before she had a chance to point out her grandfather, Ann burst in with, 'Hey there is my grandpa.' She pointed to the other end of the same row. That guy had a smaller horn, but a bigger hat.

"That is my grandpa J. Doll," Ann announced.

Two grandpa J. Dolls in the same band!

The ladies started a verbal waltz. No it was more of a fox trot, and it was fast. I got lost.

This band was highly polished. It had been growing and improving for thirty years.

The original band was started in 1860 something. The first Fourth of July to be celebrated in the village was to have a parade, the bigger the better. Five guys hit on the idea of a marching band. They had a trombone, a saxaphone, a clarinet and a drum. My goodness, the Drum Major had a high luxuriant head piece and a marching staff or baton. With three days of practice, they were ready to send beautiful music clear to heaven.

The great day arrived. The new marching band was placed near the middle of the parade.

It was awe inspiring! Simply beautiful until they came to Second Avenue. The parade turned left. The band turned right. The Drum Major was still in step and swinging his baton, until Hans Goubermier's dog rushed out and bit him in the leg. That upset the leader. As he lay on the street, the other members stumbled over him. They got sorted out in a big rush to keep their position in the parade. Otto Selinger happened to get his sheet music back in the holder upside down. That little error made for a big discord.

That was the very start of the brass band. Giant Oaks from little acorns grow.

Pigeon

When the last wooden candy pail was used, I would not dare guess. The first one that I saw was at a ball game when I was five years old. That was a long time ago. The pail was round with a flat bottom. The boards that formed the sides were a quarter of an inch thick. The wood in the bottom was just a trifle thicker. There were two bands of wire twisted around the pail to hold the wood in place. There was a wire handle to carry it with. The pail would hold about three gallons of candy. Some country stores had a group of these pails on a counter, each with a different type of candy.

The word had gone out early in the week. Bring your shot guns. There will be a pigeon shoot at Ben Nybo's after church on Sunday.

Albert Nybo was the pigeon procurer and the Shoot Marshall, if he had a title for the day.

There were two creeks with wooden bridges spanning them. One was four miles north and the other was ten miles south. With the help of three others in their late teens, the Pigeon gather began. They drew straws to see who went to the nearest bridge and who went to the south bridge. Some kind of a weed stem or straw was held in a hand with only the tips showing. Each team captain drew a straw. The short straw was the loser. The two guys that had the long straw took the team and wagon to the north bridge. For equipment they had a long stick, four horse blankets, a barn lantern and the cluck cage. The cluck cage was a wire mesh thing about three feet long and a foot square with a little sliding door in one end. Its real purpose on the farm was to hold a chicken in there for a while. If a hen would not set on her nest of hatching eggs or not lay eggs, she was put in the cluck cage to meditate for a few days and hopefully give up her errant ways.

The cage was loaded into the wagon and two guys drove north to the bridge. It was near pitch dark so they were as silent and quiet as possible so they would not scare the birds. They hung the horse blankets on the sides of the bridge. When the lantern was lit the two pigeon hunters entered the cosy little sleeping quarters of the birds. With the long stick they disturbed the pigeons. As the birds were caught, they were hustled into the cluck cage.

The fellows that went to the south creek had similar ideas, but they had water under the bridge to contend with. They got a few pigeons.

Sunday morning Albert carefully pounded a fence staple into the bottom of the pail. Carl held the pail over the post maul. That was done to support the flimsy wood while the staple was driven half of its length into the pail. The end of a hundred foot long piece of string was tied to the staple. When all was ready, the pail was set upside down with a Pigeon underneath. The mark on the ground was a hundred feet from the pail. The Marshall and the shooter were side by side. When the shooter was ready he would call 'Pull'. The guy beside him would give the string a jerk, the pigeon would either fly away or just its spirit would depart.

Sunday afternoon arrived and so did the neighbors with their shot guns. They drew numbers out of a hat to establish their turn to shoot. Abe Tomlinson got spot number one, and Ben Nybo got the last spot. In between were Herman Nybo, Jack Carswell, Ben Newton, Ole Stormyr and possibly others.

Abe shot first, and he got his pigeon. Most of those that followed were successful. Ben Nybo had a clean miss. The second round was much like the first.

Ben stood with his double barreled shot gun loaded. When he said pull, he also pulled both triggers on his gun. Albert standing with the string in his hand beside his father said, "Dad, you did not give the pigeon time to get away from the pail." Then to his helpers, "Turn the pigeons loose. The shoot is over until we get to Herbert and get another pail of candy."

To quote one of the men that were there, "When Ben let fly with both barrels of his 12 gauge, the pigeon and the pail were all shot to hell."

Yu Fix Muy Truck?

The truck was six years old. It was bright blue without a dent or scratch. There were weak spots in the paint on the front fenders. It was nearly rubbed off.

The little old guy that drove it to the Truck Branch & Body Shop looked to be more used up than his truck. His bib overalls were well worn, and his shirt was faded. His face was roundish. There was something odd about his eyes. They did not quite focus. And, he was short one front tooth. His smile was friendly, but he was a bit hard to understand. His mother tongue was not English.

He asked the shop foreman, "Can yo up fix muy truck."

"What is the trouble with your truck?"

"Motor he is good not."

"OK we can check it out."

The next afternoon our customer was back.

He was told, "Your engine is in poor condition. What do you want us to do?"

He did not hesitate, "New one in put."

Fritz, the general manager, and Jim the credit manager, were both there to back up James, the shop foreman, for that deal.

James carried on. The other two were in the background.

"International Trucks have three quality engines. Red Diamond, Blue Diamond or Gold Diamond . (I am not sure that I have the colors in their right order, but here they are.) The Red is the cheapest, Blue is next and Gold is the brand new factory type engine. The Gold is much more expensive than either of the other two."

"Go Gold," the truck owner said.

There was a hurried little get together of the three company people.

Fritz, "More business in selling the Gold."

Jim, "The bank says he is a solid customer."

James, "Yes sir, we will get the new engine for you as soon as we can."

The little old man, "Goot' Gumbuy."

This fellow was like the Will-O-The-Wisp. Now you see him, now you don't. He kept a sharp eye on the progress of his truck.. When the engine was removed and the job at a stand still, he thought that would be a good time to do the steering. That called for king pin sets and tie rod ends, well the whole works. While the new engine was coming from the factory, the transmission, deferential and brakes were serviced or replaced. The engine and exhaust pipe and muffler were replaced when the new engine came from the factory.

The truck was finished, the bill was presented, and then the fur hit the fan.

The beginning of the International truck deal started a week before we ever saw the little old man.

This little old guy was a supreme actor. He also must have had a grudge against the garage.

He was going to deal his Chev half ton on a better vehicle. His old truck was being road tested and appraised for trade in value. He inspected everything on the used car lot. His neighbor was parting with his International truck. Our man was looking at the car next to where the salesman was telling why they could not allow much for the International truck. As he listed the faults to the owner, our little old guy had his back turned, but his ears were wide open.

The neighbor signed the deal and drove his new purchase away. Our man still listened.

"This clunker looks good. It needs a can of additive in the motor oil to smooth out the noise. And we'll put five new tires on and we will sell it for a thousand dollars with the premium guarantee." So said the sales manager.

The hero or scoundrel of this story then walked down town and back. The International was getting the last new tire installed.

"If you give me good price for Chev, I take that one."

After some tight negotiations he payed a couple of hundred dollars and drove away in the Blue International. What was more important, he had the fifty-fifty signed guarantee in his pocket.

The people at the truck branch had never seen this truck and had no idea that it was a Good Will Guaranteed used truck. As far as they knew this was just a customer off the street.

His truck was ready,and the cashier said , "That will be exactly fourteen hundred dollars, Sir."

The little pudgy guy lost his foreign accent, 'With this guarantee it will be seven hundred dollars."

"Just a minute. I'll have to call Jim."

Jim was soon on the scene, "Oh no, we cannot accept the guarantee for all of that work."

The customer asked to use the phone. He dialed a number and talked.

"George, this is Max. That little deal we talked about today when I was in your law office, well it is here now." He listened for a minute, and said to Jim, "You should get this."

"Hello, Jim, this is George. You remember me. We met in court last month. Max has a bonafide certificate. If you will not honor it for half of the bill , we will see you in court.

The deal was closed for seven hundred and all guarantee certificates were withdrawn and rewritten to the advantage of the company.

Sheep and More Sheep

They were the youngest of the Muri boys. Being a pair of industrious workers, they were offered farm jobs. The going wage was $10 a month.

Dave owned a beat up old tin Lizzy Ford. Ted patched up enough old tires to get them to Alberta. Bright and early on a morning in May, 1931, they pointed the old car west. Somewhere along the trail they picked up Carl and Buster. The foursome reached Medicine Hat, Alberta that night. With a seventy-five cent hotel room, followed by a fifteen cent breakfast, they would top off the radiator, and be on their way. There was a water tap at the back of the hotel where they had parked the car. Ted and Carl were pumping up a tire. They had their very own rusty water pail. David was using it to fill the rad with water. A city cop checking for skulduggery in the back lane that early morning had lots of questions. David was slowly winning on the radiator, so he did not stop. Teddy was right there with all of the answers that any officer might want.

"What is your name?" the cop asked.

"Theodor A. Muri, this is Carl and Buster, and that guy is my brother Dave."

"Where are you going."

"West."

"How far west?"

"Far enough to find work."

"Do you think that this car will get you that far?" the officer directed this one to David who was still trying to fill a leaky radiator.

"When this thing peters out, I guess we'll have to walk," David answered.

"Good luck, fellas. I hope you find work."

The old Ford with air in its tires and water in its rad, and eight gallons of gas that cost the travelers one buck, just purred along. Across the river and up the hill, they drove through Red

Cliff before the sun was high. In the early forenoon they went past Suffield. They were not traveling fast, but certainly steady. Old Tin Lizzy had four wheels, four doors, but no top. This made it so much nicer to view the countryside , and lean out to check for flat tires. They had more than enough of them.

A mile or two beyond the last town, they overtook a man walking. He accepted a ride. It seemed that he could not be drawn into the conversation. The four pals had this guy pegged as a surly beggar. They traveled west for nearly an hour, then Ted looked over the edge of the car.

"Yessir reesir, we have a flat tire." Ted nudged the hitch hiker, "Last man in has to change the tire."

The new passenger clutched his gunny sack of personal stuff, got out and without a nod started up the road, walking again.

It was a big joke to the rascals with the car, that they had the grump walking again. It was twenty minutes later that they passed the hiker again. With an arm wave he asked for a ride. Ted pointed to the rear tire, and shook his head in a NO.

The four travelers had wandered into that part of Alberta that is north of the Trans-Canada Highway. Some where near the Red Deer River they came to a sheep camp.

"Need any help?" Ted was the front man.

"Yu have to talk to shearing chief."

The next encounter went better.

"Hello, I'm Ted Muri from Saskatchewan. Do you need any shearers for your crew?"

"Well, have you sheared before?" asked the boss.

"Yes, we have thirty-five head at home. My brother and I always shear them."

"You have that many sheep at your place?"

"We sure do." Ted would not take a backseat for anything.

"You have that many, and you shear them all?"

"Why, sure we do them every spring." With that Ted started to pull in his horns. Was this guy poking fun at him and the little band of sheep.

"I am John Robbens. I am short handed so I'll give you a try for the afternoon."

The afternoon ended at sundown.

John made a few decisions. "Carl and Buster, you will never earn your soup on the shearing floor. If you want to pack wool bags, and can keep up with the shearers, you have a job. It pays a dollar a day."

Carl and Buster became wool packers.

"Dave and Ted, tomorrow I will show you how to open a fleece proper. We will see if you are strong enough to use a heeled shear. I have a number in mind, and if you can shear that many on Saturday, you are on the crew. If not it's down the road for you guys."

The next morning the first lesson was on how to sharpen the shears.

"You will do it in three strokes on the hone for each blade, when you learn how."

"Tomorrow we will go out to a wagon wheel and bend your shears so they have all the heel you can handle," so said teacher John.

"Set a sheep on its tail end, hold the jaw behind your left elbow, then open the blades about three inches . Drive the blades flat against the brisket and throat and come out at the left ear. There your fleece is open. Now shear," He sounded like a tough old boss.

By Friday both Muri boys had the lower edge of their shear blades barely touching. With a shove, not a clip, there was an eight inch stripe of fresh sheared sheep. This type of wool clipping was new to the brothers, and it did mean more sheep done each day.

Mr. Robbens, who by now was John to everyone in camp, proved to be very entertaining. With a big green leaf from a poplar tree between his lips, he could imitate almost any band instrument.

"I grew up with sheep in Utah. You had to be a Mormon to be on the crew. When I joined the first shearing crew, we had thirty-five thousand sheep to do. There were twelve of us shearing. With the herders, handlers, bag packers, teamsters that hauled the wool to the railroad, and the cooks, the camp was so big we felt like we were in a city. The sheep were small desert animals, something like the Navaho sheep. The best I ever done was one hundred and sixty-six in a day."

When John was a young man, before the turn of the century things must have been different in Utah. With John's stories, bedtime sometimes was a bit late.

Late on Saturday afternoon. John advised, "Ted stop now." Poor T.A. Muri believed that he was fired. To David he said, "You can do four more, and that is it."

They each had the same thought, "What gives with this guy? We have worked like idiots, and we still get fired?"

"Well, boys, I figured if you could do sixty sheep each by Saturday, I would want you on my crew. Here Ted has done one hundred, and Dave has ninety-six. When you get six cents a sheep it is nice if you stop at one hundred every day. That way it is easier for figuring wages."

These guys were making six dollars a day. The fellas that stayed home had to work for more than two weeks to earn that much money.

You would think that with that kind of riches, the brothers would come home with a better Tin Lizzy.

No, they came on a CPR Pullman coach. They slept in berths from Calgary to Swift Current.

Some Change

Uncle Jens came to the US before the turn of the century. In the new land he took command of his life, and anything that touched it. He obtained homestead land in North Dakota. It was a small start, but it did not stay small. He seemed to do everything right which helped to enlarge the farm.

Jens was about five foot eight, with a round face and the rest of his body was slightly rounded, too. The black mustache on his upper lip seemed to be there to help project his voice. Not that his voice needed any extra help, he talked with a deep bass rumble. His laugh, or even a grunt, was in the same deep timber.

Uncle Jens used to come to Canada to visit his sister, my Grandma. As soon as Jens and Aunt Letty arrived the old party line phone would get hot. All of the aunts and uncles with their kids would descend on Grandpa and Grandma and their guests. The ladies sat around the kitchen table, and the men would be in the living room. My cousins, Basil and Woodrow, and I were right in with the men.

Uncle Jens told that last week the hardware merchant came to the sheriff's office and told him that a certain farmer had bought a ten gallon keg of wood alcohol, and that morning he came back for another one. The sheriff and his deputy went out to the farm, and there they found the guy with the ten gallon wooden keg on his shoulder pouring it into the cream separator. The hired man was on the crank turning the machine. The sheriff asked him why he was doing that, and the farmer said that they threw away what came out the cream spout and drank what came out the milk spout. The sheriff did not know of any law that said you could not drink wood alcohol.

Woodrow asked, "What is wood alcohol ?"

Jens answered, "It is stuff that when you light a match to it, it will burn with a blue flame."

Woodrow's question was, "What would happen if he lit a cigar?"

"Oh, I suppose he would have a blue flame at each end." Jens was never stuck for an answer.

Then there was the time they took the new grain buyer out snipe hunting. The hunt had to start with the new hunter buying a keg of beer. He sat in a hole in a snow bank, holding a gunny sack and froze, while the rest of the snipe hunters drank up his beer. Then there was the time the bank manager pulled a dirty deal on someone, so on the fourth of July, a group of farmers got the bank manager in the horse trough at the livery stable, and scrubbed him clean. The banker got pneumonia. There was a lot of trouble over the stunt.

One of the mothers would come and say, "It is school tomorrow for you guys, so go and lie on Grandma's bed. We moved down and sat on the floor in the corner. The stories and laughter would carry on. The same lady would come back and check up on us kids. With a word or two to the men, she would leave. From then on the talk was in Norwegian, and the laughing was even richer. How absolutely disgusting! The three of us would go out to sleep in some car.

Years passed, and Uncle Jens came again. The laughing was like always. Some new stories, some reaching way back, but that was Jens, and they were all good.

"Since we got into the war with you guys against Hitler and Mussolini, things have sure changed. We have some very smart men in our government, but some of our congress men are duds. They are like an old lady when the hawk flies over the chicken coop. They just stand and wring their hands, or do some dumb thing to look important. They appointed me Grain Controller of North Dakota. I have an office in Washington and a secretary. I have to get on the train and go to the office twice a year. There is nothing to do, and Mary, the secretary, is a smart girl so she can handle it.

I got a letter that said every patriotic civil servant should turn in their cars to help the war effort. So now I am a civil servant, and I will part with my 1941 Chevrolet sedan. It is like new, but then I will be in line for a new car as soon as we lick Hitler and his Nazis. This is my last trip with this car.

We have the 1939 pickup and that will take Letty and I to church or to town. Melvin can do his courting with the truck. That way he might find a farm girl to marry."

Uncle's next trip to Canada was in the spring of 1946. He was driving a brand new Red Ford Convertible with a White Top. He sure made a big splash with us young guys.

One day he drove near the South Saskatchewan River to visit his old friend Ole. These two had played together as kids in the old country. The red car stopped and Ole came out and they shared an old-time hand shake. Jens opened his jacket and brought out two long fresh cigars. Ole not only refused the smoke, but gave a lengthy sermon on the evils of tobacco. Jens did not know that his old buddy had joined a church that followed a more rigorous path to the hereafter.

It still did not occur to Jens that Ole had changed religions. He tapped the button on the instrument panel, the glove box door opened and he drew out a bottle of whiskey. Ole got real warmed up on the evils of drink. This was the start of a big lecture.

Jens interrupted, "Ole, if you chewed snuff and ate hay, you still would not be fit company for man or beast."

The red convertible left the farm and left Ole standing in a cloud of dust.

In The New Land

This item may not be historically correct. It was told to me many snows ago. I enjoyed it then so here it is.

J.J.Jones was a young man from Wales. Moose Jaw, Saskatchewan was as far as he dared go. His money was dwindling and if he traveled farther west, it would just cost that much more. As he stood on the side walk near the railway station, he made up his mind. He had to make a living so why not start right here.

The year was 1905 and Moose Jaw was a bustling city. On the Main Stret they even had wood blocks on end for their side walks. Young Mr. Jones saw the error of this construction. When the ground thawed in the spring, some of the blocks would raise and it may be hard walking on an uneven surface.

J.J. opted for a traveling outfit rather than look for a job in the city. A small hammer headed blue roan horse with an economy built saddle, he bought for thirty-five dollars. Jones did not realize that his new horse was a retired cow pony that had learned the cow business on some ranch.

A wool blanket and a canvas tarp a bit bigger than the blanket and a meager food supply were tied on the back of the saddle. He was ready for the open road and darn near broke. What money he had left was no problem to carry.

The jeers and insulting remarks about the scrawny Englishman and his scrawny horse were considered very funny by the guys at the livestock area of the city.

The first half hour of riding west from Moose Jaw was rather aimless. It was a shock for the Welshman to find that his poor horse going a fast walk had a motion much like a rocking chair. The saddle was another item. It rubbed where ever it touched him.

The open country and being alone was much preferred to the smart talk back at the cattle pens. In the evening Jack stopped by a pond left in the creek bed by the spring run off. He tied his horse to stone that could be moved with a hard pull on the halter shank. The animal could reach more grass, but would not get too far away. Jack ate enough to drive away the hunger pangs and made his bed on the open prairie and looked up at the stars.

The second day Jones rode to the top of the highest hill west of Moose Jaw. From there he surveyed the world of prairie grass around him. Rolling hills covered with grass in every direction as far as the eye could see. All morning Jones had encountered small bunches of cattle.

Later he met a man on horse back. After greetings and small talk Jackie Jones asked him,

"Are any of these cattle for sale?"

"No, not from our ranch. In a few months we will round up a herd and take to Moose Jaw and sell them there."

Mr. Jones saw the reasoning behind that line of thought. Anyone that close to market would be hard to buy from. He kept his horse heading west. In time he went by Old Wives Lake and still carried on chasing the sunset.

It was mid morning when J.J.Jones rode into the Turkey Track Ranch yard.

The greeting, "Get down and come in." was strange but welcome. He had gotten around a huge steak dinner. It sure beat his travel meals.

"Mr. Cruikshank, would you consider selling me ten of your steers on credit?"

"What would you do with ten head of steers?" the rancher asked.

"I would walk them to Moose Jaw, sell them and come back and pay you," Jones replied.

Mr. Cruikshank thought this over. 'A green horn Englishman walking ten steers to Moose Jaw. Impossible. But what would there be to lose? Within a couple of days the steers would be back on their home range again. They would get away on this guy the first or second night.'

"All right, come into the office and I will have to give you a bill of sale for the ten head."

The rancher with two riders and young Mr. Jones rode up on the high land south of the ranch headquarters. There ten steers were cut from the herd. Jones was glad to see that every animal had distinctive marks. They were picked that way by the ranch people so they would be easy to spot when they came home again.

"You two fellas help Mr. Jones for about six miles, as far as the small lake north of the high ridge. Good luck, Mr. Jones." Mr. Cruikshank could smile and picture the life of the steers for the next few days.

At what is now known as Gaspers Lake, the ranch boys said goodby. J.J pushed the steers hard for the next four hours. The sun had gone down when he came to a good spot for the night's camp. He had followed a creek some miles. There was an intersecting stream with straight banks that flowed into the main creek. It took a two mile detour upstream to cross the little stream with high banks. He crossed and turned south again. In a tight little triangle where the two streams met, the night camp was made. Jackie had the steers near the creek banks. The horse was tied as before to a heavy rock. The camp fire was half way between the two creek banks. The steers bedded down. They were tired. Jones spread his meal time out over the night. He would doze, wake up and look at the steers lying so quietly. Doze again, wake up, chew a bit o dried meat, and doze again.

The sky was beginning to lighten in the east. Jones saddled up his horse and had the cattle moving in the direction of Moose Jaw. He pushed the steers fast until noon then let them graze and fill up. Night time found them along the north edge of Old Wives Lake. There again the young man spent more time watching his livestock that he had bought on credit, than he did sleeping.

On the fourth day the red steer with the white patch on his rump got homesick. He started on the back trail. The horse turned very quick to follow. That was J.J. Jones's first hurricane ride. Both steer and horse were going fast. All Jones could do was to grab the saddle horn and hang on. The blue roan horse reached over and took a bite out of the steer's rump. What an outlandish beller! The animal cried blue murder and rushed back to join the rest of the herd. That ended the mutiny.

Seeing that there were scattered herds of cattle in the higher hills, Jones moved his around to the flatter land north of the hills. He spent the next week edging his stock closer to the city. The cattle seemed to like the slower pace. They filled out and even regained some of the weight that they lost in the first days of travel.

Early one morning the ten steers with the Turkey Track brand stood at the gate of the cattle pens on the southwest side of Moose Jaw.

"There is a crazy Englishman out here with some Turkey Track steers. What shall we do?" one of the yard men asked his boss.

A person would have to be a little off the beam to steal these steers and bring them right to the stockyards. The boss went to investigate.

Mr. Jones handed over the bill of sale. The boss man read and re-read the paper. With a smile he saw Cruikshank's idea of a joke, but it seemed to have backfired. He inspected the steers.

"What happened to this one with the sore beside his tail?"

"He was trying to get away so my horse bit him," Jackie answered.

"Your horse is colored somewhat like a badger. He must be quite a digger."

That was the moment that J.J. Jones and his horse Digger became cattle dealers.

On the way back to pay Mr. Cruikshank, Jones scouted a trail that was south of Old Wives Lake. He arranged to keep his cattle in a rancher's corrals over night. That was the night that he could have a solid sleep and be more rested for the last half of his cattle drive.

In the following three years J.J. bought as many as thirty animals at a time from Cruikshank.

By the time the Saskatchewan government had opened the land west of Moose Jaw for homesteading, J.J.Jones had ridden his horse, Digger, over most of it.

I was just a kid moving two horses along the road northeast of Hodgeville, Saskatchewan. I rode past a farmyard that was so neat and well kept. There was a wind break of tall trees on three sides and only well kept bushes and hedges on the south side facing the road. That farm had a white two story house and a huge red barn. There was a driveway on the side of the barn that let the owner haul a load of hay right up into his loft.

In large green letters on the roof of the barn was the name J. J. Jones.

Bush Pilot

Christenson's Auto Body was the place. Norman Laventuer was the shop foreman and I (Bernie) was the boss. To start each day Norman got the coffee maker in action. At ten o'clock we took our coffee break. Usually we were not alone for that bit of time. Tom of The Royal Canadian Mounted Police, if he was in town or passing through, or some other interesting person would join us for a cup of coffee.

One day it was Dale Blair that stopped in. Dale is a retired bush pilot. The lakes and rivers of northern Saskatchewan were known to Dale like a post man would know the houses on his route.

Joe hoped to hire Dale to help tie up the deal on some mining claims in the north. Each claim was staked and on a certain day they would be eligible for filing the claim. The filing would consist of flying twenty men up to the camp on the edge of a certain lake.

"How is the camp equipped?" Dale asked.

"Every thing you need is right there." Joe assured him.

"Is there a tent?"

"Yes, it is set up with food and bedding."

"How about snow shoes?" Dale asked.

"You won't need snow shoes. The claim stakes start right at the edge of the lake where the camp is."

"Is there fire wood there?"

"Oh yes, all cut and dry, right beside the tent. There is another camp at the far side of the claim stakes. It is all set up, too."

Dale thought it over and said, "You go down to the office and pay for the flight in and out. Then get your crew together. I will have to start at noon to get them all flown in to-day."

"I will give you enough money to pay each man twenty dollars as a tip when you unload at the airport. I will give you food for them to eat on the way out." Joe made it sound more than halfway good.

The plane would take seven men at a time so that would be three trips in and as many back out. It was an hour north of LaRonge and the days were not that long even though it was late in the winter. At five minutes to seven o'clock the next morning there was to be a man at each claim stake to write his name and the time on it. The first guys in were to go to the farthest camp and wait for daylight.

The guys on the early flight got out of the plane and when I was airborne I circled and I saw the men were not stopping at the main camp. There must have been some old prospectors in the group. They went right into the forest.

The second bunch were taken in. When I came with the last flight, the second group were standing around a miserable little camp fire in front of the tent.

It was after sundown when I cut the motor on the plane. There would be no more flying until daylight.

I inspected the camp. No fire wood. Three blankets. No food. No snow shoes. To make things worse the closest claim stake was a mile from the lake.

The food for the trip home was brought out that night. It was forty-two ham sandwiches for twenty-one of us. At the far camp there was only a small tent and nothing else. We had no choice but to spend a miserable night out in the north country. When the crew was gathered up it sounded like we were going on a moonlight picnic. We were not a bunch of happy campers.

We had to climb a high ridge to go from the lake to the claim stakes. The snow was waist deep, and I said before, no snow shoes. There was the oldest man in the group that was having trouble navigating in the deep snow. I helped him to the top of the ridge and left him at stake number one. I took stake number two. At five minutes after seven we signed our names and the time and date on the claim stakes.

We were finished the job and for the trip home it was a case of first one in first one out.

It was twelve o'clock noon when the last group were back in town. As luck would have it there right in front of the hotel I met Joe.

"Did you get them stakes all signed?" he asked me.

"We sure did."

"Where are the boys ?" Joe wanted to know.

"They are in the beer parlor."

"I should go in and buy them a round of drinks," Joe figured.

"No, don't go in there now. If you do they will kill you," Dale advised him.

"What was wrong? Was the camp not good enough? Did you have enough money to give each one his twenty?" Joe seemed quite concerned.

"There was no camp and no food and no snow shoes and the snow was waist deep. Every one got paid and I still have one hundred and fifty dollars of your money and after yesterday's deal you will have to kill me before you get it back."

Alfred Taylor

Alfred was a street orphan in England. It is likely that he was taken in by the Dr. Bernardo Home Society. He was sent to Canada at a very early age. He worked for his keep on a farm in Ontario. While there his life was valued to be slightly less than a slave. When he was in his early teens, he left the farm. When he came to Saskatchewan is lost in time. He was in the Regina area for some years. Hodgeville was the next stop that we know of.

The years of hunger and malnourishment as a child had shortened his mental growth. He was kind, considerate, and a good person in general. Sometimes he did not complete his thoughts but he went right ahead anyway. He worked for Sidney Muri in the Hallonquist area for a few years. From there he moved to Moose Jaw where he was employed at a café, pealing potatoes.

Alfred was given his meals, plus a small wage to pay for his room, and a few dollars to spend. He had never had it so good.

At Hodgeville Alfred Taylor worked for Doc Michials. One spring day he was sent to harrow a field of wheat. The team consisted of three old mares and a young stallion. His orders were 'Every two rounds, stop and rest the horses and check the harrow, make sure all of the teeth are still there, make sure that the harness is still on the horses.'

The stallion was resting, but being a young male, had extended his organ. Alfred made a loop in the end of a team line. With a backhand flip he caught the thing. Now the horse gave up his day dream in a hurry. He retracted the male part that he had out in the sunshine. The end of the line was drawn in as well.

Alfred had a problem. The slip knot that he had just tied was somewhere inside of the horse, somewhere between his back end and his ears.

Mr. Taylor needed help. He drove the horses up to a nearby sagging barbwire fence. He tied the old mares to the top wire, and separated the stallion from the team. He had not stopped to reason that the entire harrow outfit would have to be taken apart by hand, and set up facing the field.

Alfred led the horse back to the farm yard. Mr. Michials was working in the blacksmith shop.

"Hey, Boss, I've got the stud here." Alfred announced.

"How did you bring him in?" Michials asked.

"Oh, simple, each end of the line on each end of the horse."

All Neighbours

Old Simon Harris was a different kind of a man. Soft, sensitive and humorous. There was his house beside the road, just after you crossed the bridge on the Pelican reserve. Simon was a classy dresser, tall and portly. He always wore a good suit jacket and a half wore out pair of running shoes.

Surrounding the town of Leoville, Saskatchewan are three reserves. Simon is on the one to the northwest called the Pelican or Chitek reserve.

"One day Ralph Woods take me to North Battleford to get his new hay tractor. The new tractor all red, he tell me it go twelve miles. I out of town and Ralph go by me in truck. I stop and push nickel that one place by spring then it go twenty five miles. Going fast got much time, go to Jack Fish Lake and see Jack same name as me but no related. I have bottle of good whiskey. Jack he want to come home to me. He stand on hitch and hold on seat. It dark on Birch Lake road. Tractor got good lights see holes and logs on road in forest. Two o'clock at Ralph's no whiskey. I wake Ralph up. Take us home. He say go sleep in bunkhouse take home in morning. Me and Jack walk, much dry. I carry new jug wine. Jack no know it on tractor. He say, "Simon gimme drink." We walk mile. Jack say Simon poor friend no drink. We open jug walk more mile. Much tired we sleep."

There were onlookers and blank spots in his story as Simon and Jack were sleeping.

Douglas Rabbitskin came by with the school bus. He saw the tired travelers having a nap, and a half a jug of red wine.

"Simon will need that when he wakes up." Douglas drove away.

Levi was the next on the scene. He came from the south, the jug was hidden from his sight, but he saw two Indian bodies lying in the grass. He lost no time getting down to the Penn store. From there he phoned the RCMP in Spiritwood.

"There are two dead Indians lying on the reserve road six miles west of the highway.

The bright sun had not had time to take the dew off the grass before the Mounties were there with two panel trucks.

Simon enjoyed this part.

"The cops come with two trucks and have boards with wheels. They tie Jack on one and me on other one. Then I sneeze wake up." Cop hollered, "Hey dis guy not dead. Try dat guy."

"Jack no dead too. We go jail in Spiritwood. Stay one day. I go to court at thirty days. Judge fine me sixty-seven dollar and keep my wine."

He shook his head and had a long sad face at the memory. "We all neighbours and Levi never even come to court."

What a breach of etiquette.

Bilingual

Our overnight guests, Duane and Shirley, were a pleasure to see. It had been a few years since we had a chance to visit into the night. One thing that they mentioned was the poodle they sheltered while its owners holidayed in Quebec. This smart little dog did not understand English. Her name was something like Fifeee.

"With my very limited French cuss words, I could make her mind sometimes. But you could swear your head off in English at her and it was like pouring water on a duck," he said.

That recalled another bilingual situation I have heard of .

Debbie Revit was the lab technician at the hospital at Ile a la Crosse, Saskatchewan. The fact that she weighed just over one hundred pounds and had one leg that had to be favored, did not help her on that night.

Angilique was a Chipewyan lady. Her home was on the shore of a lake at the very north edge of Saskatchewan. This Chip gal weighed in at well over three hundred pounds. Yes, she was a big girl. She had suffered a back injury. When the Medics way up north loaded her on the plane, she was told,
' relax the best you can and do not move at all.'

The Beaver aircraft touched down at 2AM, Sunday morning. Debbie was called in to do an emergency x-ray, at 2AM Sunday morning. Angie's trip from the float dock to the hospital, took the same time as Debbie's trip to the lab. They met at the hospital lab. Now for help to move Angie from the stretcher to the x-ray table.

At closing time at a bar room a few guys that liked to carve people, got their knives out and went at it. They arrived for patches and repair at the emergency ward moments after Debbie and Angie got there.

Help in the x-ray lab was not available. They had gone to administer health and comfort to the bleeding knife wielders.

Angie was true to her instructions that had said DON'T MOVE. Debbie got the wheeled stretcher beside the x-ray table, and moved one leg of the patient to the table. That in itself was a big job. Angie's leg weighed more than all of Debbie. When she tried an arm the leg got off the table again.

On her papers it stated that Angie's language was Chipewyan. English was just so much gibberish to the native lady.

In total exasperation Debbie let slip a French swear word, the vilest profanity in the French language. Angie chuckled, much to the girl's embarrassment. She spoke in French and Angie answered. Debbie was bilingual, French and English. Angie, too, was also bilingual, French and Chipewyan.

When they both spoke the same language, the transfer to the x-ray was done by the two girls alone.

That swear word that Debbie's mother was sure that her girl did not even know, was the key to a firm friendship.

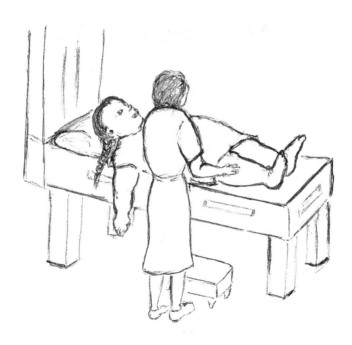

Wheat

The tall wooden grain elevators that cleared the sky line of every prairie town or village were built when wheat was king. The land was new, so were many of the land owners.

With every one of those tall buildings there was a small office. The company's agent would sit in the office until a farmer brought another load of wheat. That was what our parents told us kids.

In reality the agent had many things to do in that office. There were shelves with books that were filled with information about the grain business. The agent or grain buyer as he was called, could spend countless hours if he was to know everything about the job. There was one book telling how to grease the elevator, another on calculating the tons in a carload if the grain was light weight. There were charts galore that stated the price of all different grains. There was the company code book. In those days all messages were by mail or telegraph. For telegrams or wires as they were referred to, there was the code book. The telegraph company charged so much per word. That is where the code book came in.

Head Office Winnipeg

Kneebone

Local Agent

The message was, "I can buy this wheat, and ship it in January."

The answer came back.

Local Agent

Puddle

Head Office

It said, "Buy this grain but weigh it in the elevator, then report to us."

These words and their meanings were in the code book. These one word messages saved a great deal of money for the company.

The grain buyer had to deal with the people that grew the wheat. It was a very rare case that led to hard feelings. There was a reason why a farmer dealt with a grain company.

Uncle Andy Tonjum had to test grain for moisture content. If it was wet, it would become moldy and spoil in the elevator. Damp or tough grain as it was called had to be elevated from one bin to another until it was dry enough to ship out. In the days of threshing machines, tough grain was not often encountered. The grain buyer had no moisture tester. It was not like today when farmers have such a devise built right into their combines.

For moisture testing Andy would try his jack knife blade on a soft wood board. It had to be sharp enough to whittle the wood , but not sharp enough to shave with. Laying a few kernels of grain on a hardwood board, he would cut across a kernel. If the two parts of the kernel just lay on the board, it was tough. If the kernel snapped away from the blade when cut, it was good. If the pieces jumped away, it was dry and could not be in better condition.

Dick Coward's reason for hauling to Andy Tonjum was, "It was seven minutes from the time I turned off the main road till I was back there again. Andy would see me coming and have the grain ticket made out , all but the weight of the grain. I would drive in the elevator and get off the wagon. Andy would weigh the load and wagon, and then turn the lift handle. The front of the wagon would raise. I would open the end gate, and the grain would pour out. The lift handle was turned the other way, the wagon came down, I got in and drove away. He would finish the ticket as I drove away. It was a nip and tuck thing to get back to the threshing outfit and change my four horse team to a full wagon and go again. If I was late it would mean a lot of shoveling wheat to clean up a mess. Tom was in the first elevator. He was good, too, but he had been a concert pianist. If I had hauled to him, I could wear out my shovel."

Art Resvick told, "When I was transferred to the Vogel elevator, the first customer I got was my brother-in-law. I weighed his wheat and made out the ticket. When he saw that I had graded his wheat as number three, he screamed and jumped a foot high. He did not like to sell his wheat at such a low grade. If it was graded number one, it would have given him a few dollars more for the load. I poured his wheat back into his truck and he drove away. In less than an hour he was back. He showed me his ticket. He had sold his wheat in Hodgeville, only a couple of miles down the road. I looked at his ticket and dug his canceled ticket out of my waste basket."

"Do you see any difference?" I asked.

"You darn right. I got number one for that load."

I said, "Look a little farther."

He did, and then he roared and nearly jumped two feet in the air. "They weighed me short, over eight hundred pounds."

"Yes, they gave you number one grade, and you gave them fifteen bushels of wheat." It was hard for me not to smirk.

The customer said, "All I want is an honest deal. I believe I will get it here."

Welly Graham had a customer that was scared to death of being charged too much dockage. Every time he brought in grain, Welly would screen out a measured sample. After weighing the weed seeds, he would check the dockage chart and it was usually five or six percent. The farmer always thought that it should be less.

The first load that the guy brought in of the new crop, Welly did not take a test for dockage. He just made out the ticket. The fella put it in his pocket and went back to his combine. A couple of days later he came back and wanted it made over for a cash ticket.

Welly looked at the ticket he had made out before, "Yes, I can change this ticket." With a bit of figuring he said, "You will owe me thirty-four dollars."

This fella was stunned, "What?"

"Because I took one hundred and twenty-five percent dockage right off the bat. Now we won't have to argue for the rest of the crop year."

The fella saw the joke. They got along better after that.

Andy had finished loading a boxcar or railcar of wheat. He noted the car number and put the seal on the door. The west wind was howling. It was so strong that it had a big Russian Thistle high in the air. To save climbing up to set the brake on the boxcar, he laid a piece of wood in front of a wheel. He went past the CPR station and handed the agent the bill of lading for the carload of wheat. Then he went home for lunch. At home Aunt Edna informed him,

"Brother George was just here with Ira Laflure. Those clowns are going to drive to Ole Stormyr's on the rail road track. It would serve them right if they got caught."

It happened that Edna's clowns had just turned off the railway, when, swoosh, a lone boxcar whistled past.

Ole phoned the CPR station to report a runaway boxcar, going past his place fast.

Andy, back from a quick lunch, missed his boxcar. The wind had rocked it until the wood was cut off. The track sloped down for fifteen miles, and the wind hurried the loaded car along.

Andy sat in the CPR station rather tense. The wires came in.

Runawy car just went through Kelstern, going east fast.

Like seconds later .
Runaway car went through Shamrock going east.
The last telegram.

Engine backed out from Moose Jaw. Saw car, stopped, drove east. Car bumped the engine lightly and hooked on. Now east of Courval going home.

"That car was supposed to go to Fort William. It's no sense to bring it back here." And, Uncle Andy went back to work.

Black Diamond

The ferry is still plying its way back and fourth across the Red Deer River. The ranch was seven miles upstream. The country school must have been on the south side of the river. That would put it up on the flat land up above the valley. The ranch land away from the valley was not rough and broken with hills and coulees, although it is not exactly flat.

Uncle Ted Muri was one of the ranch hands. His job was to ride for miles every day.

He and I were leaning on the rails, looking at a half a dozen of his horses in the corral.

"To look at that trim black gelding over there reminds me of the schoolmarm's horse ." The far away look in uncle's eyes told that he was thinking back over the years.

"At the ranch, we had this horse that was the best natured animal that I ever broke to ride. He was a keen black gelding. The only name he had was The Black.

Well, the school teacher came to the ranch to board. I suppose that the ranch house had more spare room than any of the farm houses in the area. That was in 1931 when it was even hard to heat the houses out on the bald prairie. Anyway the teacher would be glad to ride back and forth to school if there was a saddle horse along with the bed and board.

The teacher was a darn nice looking girl. If I had not fell like a ton of bricks for the store keeper's sister, Pauline, I may have been interested. She was no stranger to a horse and was a good rider. Black was the best horse for the teacher to use. He could make it to school on a dead run if she wanted him to, but she never treated her horse that way.

I was riding a stocky bay with black legs. I had broke him out a year before and he was a good working saddle horse. It was in February, at the supper table I mentioned that my horse was getting run down and sure could use a soft job for a week or two. Jack, the boss, kicked the idea around and asked teacher if she would trade horses with me for a while.

'I will trade Black Diamond to you for a while but you must promise to treat him right.' Teacher was willing to make the switch.

The Black was not a good enough name for her horse. She claimed that he was a diamond so he became Black Diamond.

The next morning was sunny with a warm soft breeze. Just a great day. I saddled the bay for the teacher. She hung her book bag and lunch on the horn and trotted away. Over her shoulder she called, 'Be good to Black Diamond.'

Ronald had a team hitched to the feed sleigh. Brother Dave was bringing out a team of horses for some reason or other. I mounted Black Diamond and swapped a few words with the guys. I reined the horse away from the barn and put spurs to him and said, Well Black----- the rest of it was forgotten. I was sitting on the ground. I landed on the back part of me that my chaps did not cover. My head and feet had not landed yet. There was Black standing looking at me. There were Dave and Ronald just killing themselves laughing. The horse had caught me unaware and he had bucked me off in one quick shot. Well, I had lots of riding to do so I caught Black up and got back on. I touched him with the spurs. Four jumps later I was lying on the ground again. It was worse that time. Jack was there laughing with the guys. After a bunch of smart talk, Ronald our Australian cowboy offered to show me how to ride the horse. Now I had been riding the rough stuff for quite a few years but I was willing to have Ron show me what I had done wrong. 'It was your spurs that he did not like,' Ron claimed.

Ronald got on and got off a heck of a lot quicker. He had lost his sense of humor. He put his spurs on and was going to take a bit of revenge on The Black.

Black went into the dandiest storm of bucking that Ronald had ever seen. Ron went into the air, way up in the air and come down to lie on the ground.

Jack stepped in, 'Don't rile the horse up any more than he is. Put him in the barn and, Ted, you go and get in your knot head mare to ride.'

I used the knot head blaze faced bay as my main horse for the rest of the winter."

It was Friday night and at the supper table the talk had to get around to how Ronald and I had bit the dirt.

"Oh, not my Black Diamond! He would not act like that. Tomorrow I will have to go out and see my friend," teacher stated.

Saturday morning teacher came to the barn and curried The Black. He seemed to be glad to see her. It was a nice chinook type of a day so she saddled the horse and led him out. It had thawed, and there was sloppy water in front of the barn where Ronald and I had landed a couple of times each on the day before. Teacher led Black over near a corral where the snow was still clean and deep. She swung on and was about to turn him and ride away. Bang! The first buck put the girl high in the air. She settled out of sight in the snow beside the corral fence. The heated lecture she gave us seemed to indicate that we were a bunch of dumb nuts that spoiled a good saddle horse.

Teacher rode the stocky bay with black legs for the rest of the school term.

I tried Black Diamond two different times and could that sucker ever buck. Jack finally sold him and he joined the Calgary Stampede bucking horse herd."

Uncle Ted finished the yarn:

"I don't know where he learned to buck. I guess that it was the first surprise of my spurs that triggered his other nature."

Sandy Land

When I was a young sprout, I had Grandpa Muri that was Mom's father. I had Grandpa Overbow in Iowa. He was really Grandma's husband. We used to get Christmas parcels from them in November. But I also had Grandpa Nybo. Well, he was grandpa to my Nybo cousins so I sort of edged in and took a bit of shade under his wing, too.

Grandpa Nybo and his son Knute owned a steam thrashing outfit. Knute was the boss of the machinery. The steam engine or the thrashing machine were both known to him. He knew their innermost secrets.

Grandpa Nybo looked after the men and horses. He was a natural early riser so he would feed the horses and wake up the men. He drove his horse Doc on the buggy and often toured the field where the thresher men were working. He carried a gallon jug that had a burlap bag cover sewn on. This was a drinking water container. When the jug was filled under the well pump spout the covering got wet with the cold water. The idea was that the wet burlap would keep the drinking water cold longer. It was a treat for the field pitchers to get a cold drink on a hot day. The field pitchers were men that helped the guys with the horses and bundle racks to get their load of sheaves on so they would be able to keep their turn at the threshing machine. Grandpa Nybo had everything run like clock work. He drove around to see the men in the field. Not only did he take a drink to them but at times he was known to run his buggy over a stook of grain that some field pitcher was sleeping behind and shirking his work. He accomplished that by taking an aim on the stook that the sleeper was resting behind. Whipping Doc into a gallop and running a buggy wheel over the stook would be a sudden wake up for the sleeper.

Driving in a loop, Grandpa would circle back to the employee that stood with a red face.

"Oh, I am so sorry to wake you up. You see Doc was trying to run away with me."

Now the fella knew that faithful Old Doc wouldn't run away even if he was in a horse race. Grandpa Nybo always kept things rolling.

It was in July of 1928 that Knute went to Henderson Brothers in Vanguard with the list of parts that he would need to get the Case steam engine in shape for the coming harvest.

Bill Henderson was a salesman. He convinced Knute that a new Case thresher and a new Case gasoline powered tractor would not cost that much more than the repairs for the steam engine.

"And the extra money it will cost you for the brand new threshing outfit will be an investment for your future. You will not need a steam engineer, nor two water haulers, nor fireman, or a straw monkey, no field pitchers, only six good bundle haulers. You will be able to cut the size of your crew in half." Mr. Henderson had a good sound argument.

Knute bought the smaller outfit.

The next morning Knute was having breakfast, and Grandpa came before he even had his first chaw of Club chewen tobacco.

"Did you get the repairs for the steamer? When do we start fixing it up? How soon will we be able to start threshing?" Grandpa was still in the clock work frame of mind.

"I bought a new outfit," was Knute's answer.

"A whole new outfit. How big is the steam engine?" Grandpa Nybo asked.

"We won't have a steam outfit. It is a gas tractor and a smaller thrashing machine."

"Why do we want a smaller machine?"

Knute explained that they would be able to cut so many jobs and have less men on the crew.

Grandpa realized that the hustle and bustle and the puffing and power of the Case steam engine would be lost for ever. To make matters worse, his job would be wiped out. There would be no need for him and Doc and the buggy out in the field. This blow had come so unexpectedly.

He was devastated.

He could feel the misery rising in his thoughts, "This is the break up of the Nybo thrashing outfit. You take the engine and I will keep the threshing machine. In a year or two I will buy my own steam engine and I will run my own thrashing outfit." That was Grandpa Nybo's offer. He went out, untied Doc from the gatepost and went home.

Knute advertised his Case steam engine for sale in the Western Producer, a farm news paper. It was not long until a letter arrived from Canwood, Saskatchewan. The writer wanted to know about the condition of the engine.

After a few letters back and forth, he asked Knute if he would trade the engine for one hundred and sixty acres of unimproved land in the southern part of the Canwood municipality.

Knute had no use for the old Case engine, in fact he was glad to be rid of it. There were also many stories floating around about the riches of the north country. He made the deal with the understanding that he would load the engine on a Canadian National Railway flat car and address it to Ordale, Saskatshewan. That was no problem. He ordered the flat car and when it came, he fired up the Case steam engine and drove it to Hodgeville, Sk. The loading platform was laid with heavy planks to hold the giant engine while it was being loaded on the rail car.

It took some tricky driving back and forth to get the monster positioned on the flat car.

Knute was glad that he had replaced the packing in the seal of the steam cylinder. That gave him power steering.

The train men got the flat car hooked in line with the box cars of the train. The locomotive gave a toot and rolled away. That was the last Knute saw of the Case. The last he heard of it was that it smashed through the loading platform at Ordale.

Years before the deal was made reports came from the Canwood district. The land there was as good as the Regina plains. It was black and rich soil.

Knute had made the deal sight-on-seen. When he did see his northern property a number of years later, he found that it was not the heavy loam of a few miles northeast of his land. The value that he had placed on the steam engine was very low.

It did not bother Knute that the northern Nybo land was very sandy.

Oh, yes. Grandpa Nybo never did get his new steam engine.

American Hunters

It was the last frost free night of the summer according to the T.V. weather man. That morning I was going to take a cut of alfalfa from the new seeded crop. Some people said that it would hurt the next year's crop if it was harvested in its first year. Others figured it would freeze and be lost anyway. We needed hay so I was going to cut one part of the field.

I made a quick trip to Dupont's Garage for a bag of bale twine. There was a collection of local guys around the garage.

"The geese are down from the north. There was a large flock in Pete Riemer's barley swathes when I came by this morning."

Another voiced his thought, "Soon the whole Prairie View country will be goose pasture."

Another spoke, "Geese can sure raise cain with swathes."

"It's time for the American hunters to show up," some one added.

John Bay a spry man in his late seventies spoke. "I was an American hunter at one time."

Every person turned to John with a surprised look. Mr. Bay never hunted anything.

"It was 1907 when we landed here in Rush Lake. My father had taken up land up at Prairie View. Dad met us with a wagon. He soon had it loaded with our stuff. There was just room left for Mother and some of the kids. A neighbor had a load of our settlers effects on his wagon. His hired man had a wagon with a heap of coal in the middle of the box. Us boys were to ride in the coal wagon. The trail led north west across the hay flats. Oh boy, there were a heck of a bunch of gophers all over. In Wisconsin we had squirrels that lived in trees. Here the darn squirrels had holes in the ground. Well, us boys started throwing lumps of coal at the squirrels. The coal had been heaped higher in the middle than the sides of the wagon. We were up near

Adam Sauders, and the hired man turned and saw us throwing coal at the gophers."

He hollered at us , "Hey, you American hunters,stop that."

"The peek of the coal pile was not above the sides of the box. If we could have kept on we would have unloaded all of the coal. That was when I was an American hunter."

Just Wait

About seventy years ago, at the beginning of hard times in Saskatchewan, a group of young men found enough money to buy the needs for a party, (a very cheap jug of wine). Wally borrowed his boss's coal and fuel delivery truck. That was their transportation to a farm several miles from town. The host was surprised by the arrival of the party goers. But then he was one of them. So what!

They had themselves a party. It was not such a big party after all. A few drinks, a few games of cards, a pot of coffee and the cold ride back to town.

Highway 13 was just a poor road with a number. It was less than a mile from town when a snow drift angling across the road put the truck in the south ditch. Being a coal delivery truck, it had two scoop shovels along. There would be no problem. With eight guys changing off with the shoveling, the truck would be back on the road before anyone worked up a sweat.

A car light was making its way towards the boys that were in the ditch.

"Light the lanterns and keep the guy from running in here like we did."

Two barn lanterns had been lit and put under the hood of the truck during the party. They and the horse hide robe were all the engine heater they had in those days.

With the lanterns glowing, two boys went up the road a few yards, to warn the oncoming driver. Two others stood on the road waving shovels. Four others stood in the excavated snow bank in front of the truck.

The other motorist payed no attention to the lanterns or the shovels. He stopped with a crash down in the ditch, against the coal truck. He emerged in a ferocious frame of mind.

"I am going to sue you for blocking the road," was his first thought. Then he checked the damage to his vehicle.

The hood was against the windshield and the radiator was bent over the engine. It was a real mess. "I'm going to sue you for damage to my truck, too."

About that time the boys figured that if they had had at their party what this guy had consumed, they would still be back at the farm.

The damaged vehicle was an older car that had been converted to a truck. The back seat space had been chewed away by hand and a little box had been put on the back end. This wooden box was about four feet square and sixteen inches high.

The angry owner had a farm near the International Boundary. He also had a shack and a team of thin horses in town. Every so often he would go to the farm for a load of oats to feed his horses.

While he was cursing and shouting, "Sue, sue, sue." Wally ran his hand into the oats. He pulled out a whiskey bottle and promised, "I'll just keep this until after the trial."

The oats hauler did some more swearing and took off for town on a dog trot.

The original party gang were barely out of the ditch, when the suing party came trotting with his horses. He seemed in a hurry to get his truck to town.

Wally told me that he went by the truck the next morning and there was only about a third of a load of oats left. "I don't think he fed that much to his horses, but then again a hundred bottles of smuggled booze takes some room, too."

"What did you do with the bottle after the trial?" I asked.

"There was no trial. That bottle with Kentucky Bourbon and the prancing horse on the label, sat on a shelf in the boss's office until my last day, when I went to join the Air Force."

Harvest Time

Connley Ledwedge was a big man, descended from New Brunswick lumber jacks.

Alfred Taylor was a little guy, descended from the slums of London. Early in his life he was starved, and it hindered his development.

This pair of farm workers were so kind and thoughtful. It was about 1938 that they worked for Knute Nybo's threshing outfit. Con was Albert Nybo's hired man, and he was an old time horse man. The team he drove were a team of bay broncos named Dishface and Lizzie. It took a man to drive that pair. Alfred, or Dynamite as he was nicknamed, drove a team of Knute's. The big old Clyde and the brown mare were named King and Flossy. Sometimes Dynamite did not think things out too clearly, but that was all right. King did the thinking for both of them. King thought for all three of them. Flossy did not bother to think.

The Case threshing machine was set up a three or four minute walk southeast of Albert Nybo's farm yard. At two o'clock that afternoon the yellow straw stopped flying out of the blower. The roar of the thresher stopped. There was trouble. The shiny Case threshing machine had a broken part.

Knute walked to the house and phoned Grismer's Garage at Hodgeville. In those days it was a marvel to phone from Hallonquist to Hodgeville. The Hallonquist operator would be at her switchboard. It had two neat little rows of handles on the flat desk part and on the upright there were rows of holes to plug the cords into to carry the message from one line to another. She had to call Vanguard, they called Swift Current, they called Morse, they called Hodgeville, and you still could not hear what the person at Hodgeville had said. Knute finally found out what he wanted to know.

He phoned Stella to bring the car. Then he drove her home again.

With the breakdown Con and Dynamite hurried to put their horses in the barn. Their reason was that horses should not be made to stand outside. But they were both back at the threshing machine when Knute stopped to pick up the broken parts. Con scanned the sky and found one little white cloud on the western horizon.

"By gum, boss, it could rain and them Tomilson coulees can get so muddy. Dynamite and I will go along to help push."

The two kind and thoughtful hired men were in the back seat of the blue Chev car.

The repair took much longer than expected. The little white cloud went somewhere else. There was no downpour which was good. Knute's two faithful helpers could not have pushed. They could hardly stand up. Knute stopped at the machine. It would be too late to start up after the parts were replaced.

Con and Dynamite had to go and look after their horses. On the walk to the barn they felt that they should hide things from the world at large. In their alcoholized condition that would be tough to do. Con lifted his feet abnormally high with each step, like he was going through very deep snow. The idea of snow must have hit his little buddy, too. Dynamite leaned forward like a cross country skier. He lifted his big work boots as if he was skiing, and away he went. He was leaning far forward, so the cloud of dust that he stirred behind did not choke him.

At the edge of the yard they stopped for a conference. The rest of the crew were lounging beside the house. It would be just as well if they did not know that the pair that went to push in the mud had a couple of beer in town.

Like the wisdom of Solomon, Dynamite said, "If I get too close they will smell it on me."

Con agreed. Dynamite resumed his ski shuffle but turned to the right. His circle of six hundred yards took him right to the barn door where Con had finished his majorette style walk. They went in and unharnessed their horses.

Dynamite neglected to unbuckle King's belly band. That little error caused the back pad to slip over the horses hips. The belly band was down at King's rear heels. Dynamite had a firm grip on the hames. He was confused. Why would that stupid harness not come off? King lifted one foot then the other. The harness did come off. Dynamite had put so much force into the pull on the hames, that he lost his balance, when King lifted his feet. Dynamite laid on his back on the center isle of the barn.

Con peered at him under the harness and asked, " Mister Taylor, do you suppose that you will be able to get King to lift his feet like that when you harness him in the morning?"

The harness was a mess, but the animals had been well fed.

Common Sense

In recent years there has been considerable interest in so called swath grazing by livestock people. With this system the crop is cut and left as a swath and the animals dig through the snow to find and eat it. In some parts of the Canadian west it is more successful than other areas.

The western provinces heard of this, so each spent a few thousand dollars (how many would be anybody's guess). Many studies have been done. Each report reflected that researcher attitude.

There were many things that influenced the financial workings of North America and Europe. Recovery from World War I seemed to be complete. In the late 20's money flowed like water. Flora Puckett, our highschool English teacher, said that in the cities one pastime of the younger set, was to stroll down the street in the evening and look for the highest number on a car license plate. It was fun to find a number that was as high as six digits. That was all of the room there was on a license plate. She claimed that it was even more fun if you were strolling with a boy.

Wall Street in New York was the financial center for the United States. In 1929 they said that Wall Street crashed. Really people withdrew their money from the investment houses. Stocks that were worth thousands one day were worth pennies the next day. People who had their money invested in the stock market were financially injured. To borrow money to run a factory or a store or a farm was out of the question. There seemed to be no money anywhere.

It was especially hard on the people of our area. They had only fifteen to twenty years from the time they moved onto raw prairie homesteads to get their land into production and build up a financial cushion.

Mr. Sykes Ramsden was no exception. He had been a tea blender in England. After one harvest season in Saskatchewan, he avoided farming. He bought the O.J. Johnson & Co. general store in Hallonquist. In the middle of the week he got in his winter stock of goods. He got it on the shelves Thursday and went home for the day. It had been a hard day but there was great satisfaction in having the sixteen thousand dollar order ready for the winter's sales. The next day was the so called Black Friday. Wall Street crashed, and Mr Ramsdens goods were worth only eight thousand dollars. Beside the drop in value over the coming months most of it was sold on credit that was never paid for.

The following spring the rain did not come and the wind blew harder than usual. This situation was common from the North Saskatchewan River to the Pecos River in Texas.

People in the larger cities had no jobs; therefore, had no money to spend. People on farms or ranches had nothing to sell. The combination of no rain and hard wind meant no crops or grass. The wind blew the dirt over fences in Alberta and Saskatchewan. In Kansas and Texas the wind buried farm machinery with blown dirt.

Nothing grew all summer long until a rain storm in July wet the ground. Then the Russian thistle grew like mad.

Berniece's dad, Isidore Doll, harvested as many thistles as he could stack for cow feed. Then he cut and raked another field and left it lie to be snowed over. His horses pawed through the snow and did very well on the snow softened thistle. Now that was Swath Gazing. He did not have the backing of any government research. In those day one just had to use common sense and do the best you could.

Cut Down

We sat around Bouteiller's breakfast nook that cloudy September morning. Norma had cleared away all but the coffee cups. Walt looked out the window at the threatening clouds.

"One time Bud and Joe and I were hunting Elk up where the Cataract Creek joins the Cline River. Bud was riding ahead of me, and Joe was back a fair little bit. Bud stopped his horse and raised his rifle. 'Whhissst there are two bulls in the water'. Well, Bud was on my right so he took the one on the right. I shot the other one but he dropped at the edge of the water. I did not want to have to drag him out of the river. I could see that he was moving a little bit, so I off my horse and started to reload my gun. The river was only waist deep, and out in the middle I spilled a hand full of shells in the water. I'll bet they are still there. Well, my elk got up and started up the hill. There I finished him with a clean shot. In a minute I was on him. Bud had his a little farther up. Joe was riding a grey horse. He tied him to a tree and was starting a fire because he saw that we were wet. There was a bang and Joe's horse dropped to the ground."

Joe hollered, "Someone shot my horse."

Bud and I were soon back across the Cline. We got on our horses and galloped up the trail along the Cataract . We soon come to the other hunters.

"Hey, one of you guys shot our horse."

Well, that was just after the Leduc oil wells come in and this was a party of new oil men from Calgary. The son of one fella said that he saw an animal. Their guide said shoot. So he shot Joe's horse. His father paid for the horse right there.

"We had enough work without another animal so we made camp on the spot."

"Things were not so good. We had nearly twenty parcels of Elk to pack down to where we had the truck and we were one horse short. When we had our meat all cut and parceled up, the oil men loaned us some of their pack animals and his son had to come with us to bring their horses back."

"We figured that Joe's horse was dead. Well it was the oil man's horse then because he had paid for it. There were two holes in the horse's belly. One going in and one going out. The Indian had made a patch out of leaves, grass and mud and put it over the holes. The darn horse was up on his feet the next morning..He gave it to his Indian guide."

"The oil man sent the guide out to see that the young fella would get back O K. When he met us, he said that he had taken the horse over to where his Dad lived near by. 'When you are ready to go out, go over and get your saddle and bridle.'

When the time came, we went to get the saddle. Anyway the old boy, the guide's Dad, did not know a thing about a saddle. To introduce ourselves to the old grey Indian, Bud gave him a cigar nearly a foot long. Well, Bud got out his Ronson trophy lighter. I don't recall what the trophy was for. Maybe for smoking the longest cigars. The old boy had the smoke going full blast and had a smile as big as a full moon, but did not have any idea about the saddle.

While Bud and Joe were trying to get something out of the old man. I went around behind the shack. Over behind a tree I saw a glare of the sun on shiny metal. There, partly hid by leaves and branches, was Joe's saddle, bridle and halter. I threw the saddle over my shoulder and picked up the other stuff and went back to where the guys were still trying to get information from the Indian. He still would not say anything about Joe's things. I dropped the saddle, bridle and halter on the ground in front of him. He got a sick look on his face. I reached over and grabbed the cigar out of his mouth. I threw it on the ground and stomped on that long cigar. I sure cut him down to size, and he looked like he was going to cry."

Diphtheria

Diphtheria and Lumbago are just two of what we could call old fashioned ailments. It could be that modern medicine has wiped out these sicknesses. It seems to me they are never in the news now a days. In my tender years Grandmothers and old ladies used illness as a comfortable topic of conversation over afternoon tea. At the age I was then I had the privilege of listening in on tea time talk. Sometimes I even heard the grown up men's stories.

I had listened in.

Uncle Andy, "Oh, he was a salty, sour old guy. He had a beard like a billy goat and was just as easy to get along with as an old goat."

Jim Beckwith, "It was strange that their daughter was so pretty and such a nice girl."

Uncle Andy, "It was too bad that she had to fall for that cowboy."

Jim, "Ya what was his name? My brother worked with him on a ranch down south of here."

Andy, "I never did see the guy. I only heard him called the cowboy."

Jim, "My brother said that he was as stubborn as a mule and always had to have his own way."

Andy, "I can't remember what old sour John's daughter's name was either."

Jim, "She come down with Diphtheria and was in isolation in the hospital here. The cowboy came to see her, but the doctor would not allow him in the room because the sickness was very contagious. The guy talked the nurse into having the girl come to the window and wave goodbye to him. He got on his horse to ride out of town. He came back and sat on his horse 'til the redhead waved to him from the window of the room she was in. He saw that it was the fourth window from the north on the second floor. He waited until after dark and took a ladder from the lumberyard and climbed up to her window. She opened the window, and in spite of the bitter cold they were hugging and kissing. The cold was too much for her and she died in a couple of days. The long ride into the hills in the cold gave Diphtheria a good hold on him and he died, too."

Dad had let his horses run at large for the winter. Uncle Ted rounded them up and brought them home.

I had to tell Uncle Teddy what I had heard of the red headed girl and the cowboy. Uncle Teddy had his saddle horse at our front door, he was holding the bridle reins so I knew that he would ride away real quick. So I had to condense my story. I gave him my four year old interpretation.

"Uncle Ted, did you know that the cowboy stole a ladder and climbed up to see his girl friend in the hospital. She was sick and died. He died, too, but he did not fall off the ladder," I explained.

Chicken Today, Feathers Tomorrow

Tom Mayne was ready to leave the cowboy life behind and be a motor mechanic in the city. It was a year after Adolph Hitler had shot himself and World War Two was over that Tom was in Lethbridge, Alberta.

The war had put hard pressure on nearly all manufactured goods. Engines that were not replaced kept right on wearing out. The irrigation area around Lethbridge was short on diesel engines. Tom got wind of some used engines in Calgary. The only thing to do was to go to Calgary and find the old smokers.

In the city he made enough inquiries until the engines were located. There was a section of the old Canadian Army Supply Depot that was to be cleared away. The land was to revert to the city.

Tom inspected the engines that he had heard about. They were three cylinder Allis Chalmers diesels. It looked like some would be fit to put to work with very little repair. He calculated their scrap iron value, raised the figure by ten percent and made the attending government official that offer. It was accepted.

"You will have so many days to clear everything out of this building." The government man was reasonable about the time. "And you have to clear that building as well. It goes along with the deal."

Tom was not dumb enough to stand and scratch his head with his mouth open. Every thing in the big building was a staggering amount but the little building, too. Whatever it contained may be another bonus.

In the largest building which was really just a good sized storage shed, the Allis Chalmers engines were on the floor in one corner. Stacked against the wall across from the door were wooden crates. In fact, the side of the building was hidden by boxes, each contained a brand new Wakashaw diesel engine. Piled at the wall to the right were cardboard boxes. New mufflers and exhaust pipes by the dozens. To get full circle to the door were heaps of used or cracked motor parts.

"Is all this stuff mine?" Tom asked.

The government man answered, "We are rid of that junk now. I have your money and there will be no refund. Sorry old scout, but you are stuck with the whole mess."

Different companies in Lethbridge got the same call.

"This is Tom Mayne, if you want diesels bring a truck and your cheque book."

Calgary people were invited to Tom's little sale, too.

The buyer had loaded all of the new diesel engines and traded Tom a sizable cheque. In a spare moment he found a new pick axe in his bargain shed. It did not take more than one swing with the pick and the lock was off the door of the little ten foot square shed. It was stacked to the rafters with welding rods. That meant more calls and more sales.

Tom had come to Calgary with a few hundred dollars in his pocket. Now he was ready to leave with several thousand.

All that money just called for another investment. Tom heard of a few hundred head of unwanted horses on the Bow Slope. That was the hills and pasture north of the Old Man River and south of the main highway.

There was a processing plant being built in Winnipeg, Manitoba that was going to use only horses. Fit the two together and the money in Tom's pocket could be doubled.

Tom bought the horses and a good used saddle. The stock was shipped to Winnipeg.

There the first bad news showed up. The plant was not ready for any animals. The good news was that there were fields of frozen crop standing nearby. Tom had to bargain for horse pasture.

The crop was of no value to the farmer but it seemed to be worth a lot if Tom's horses were going to eat it. A few hundred horses would do good on a field until it was eaten off. Tom would have to go and make a deal with another froze out farmer.

The plant was ready and they took a dozen horses from Tom. Then he was told that he would have to wait. A company in Calgary was sending four hundred head, and they would have to be done first. Tom had to hunt more pasture, and move his horses.

"The boys from Calgary had more clout than I had and they saw me as future competition so they broke me just as easy as that".

It was in December when Tom's horses were finally sold.

"Then I had to ride to one farmer after another to pay for my pasture bill, where my horses had harvested acres of frozen crop. The horse manure that stayed in the fields was worth more to them guys than the crop was but I was stuck and had to pay."

When I was all settled up and bought my train ticket west, I had a twenty dollar bill left."

On Christmas Eve he arrived at his wife's family home. Emerald was there. Tom greeted her.

"Here is the entire profit on the fall's dealing . It's yours."

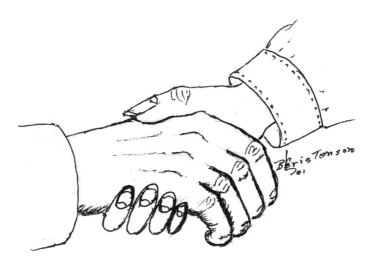

Never Say Die

It was in the spring of 1938, and I was the luckiest twelve year old kid on the face of the earth. I was allowed to go with Uncle David, when he took the young horses to summer pasture at the Saskatchewan River. Uncle Reinhart had made a deal with Fred Richardson to have the fifteen or twenty, one and two year old colts at his ranch on the south side of the Saskatchewan River, for the summer. Uncle Reinhart made the deal because most of the horses were his.

The sun broke through the clouds on that Easter Monday morning when we were at Wiwa Creek. At eleven-thirty that morning, Uncle Reinhart driving his green 1929 Chevrolet, caught up with us three miles south of Herbert. He had a basket of sandwiches, and two half gallon sealers of coffee. While the horses grazed on the dry cured grass, we ate our sandwiches. It was a full hours rest or I might not have been able to get on my horse again. I ate so much.

The sun was close to the horizon when Uncle rode around and got ahead of the colts and turned them into Norman Nelson's drive way. Our traveling stock were run into the big corral with its eight foot high board walls. Oscar and I forked hay out to our stock. Our saddle horses were put up in the barn and well taken care of.

Norman's father, Tom, had been a coach man in Norway in his teen age years. On his farm north of Herbert, he had built this huge corral, and the inside of it had seen hundreds of horses, and a fare number of mules. He made a business of breaking horses to work. A horse dealer, Mr. Jones, would go to Kansas and bring a large herd to his ranch north of Swift Current. He would bring thirty or forty head at a time for Mr. Tom Nelson to educate.

Norman was a cousin of Uncle David's, so stopping there for the night was more of a family get-together, than an along the road stopping place.

Thelma had made a big meal. We had breakfast by lamp light. As soon as we had eaten, Norman went to the blacksmith shop and lit the forage. Our horses were huddled in the corner of the corral trying to get away from the dollar sized snow flakes falling, one beside the other. When we would get a halter on a horse, we led it to the shop where Norman put a brand on its right front hoof. The brand was put on just below the hair line, and was painless to the horse.

When the branding was finished, we saddled our horses. I was told to go to the road and turn the herd north, then come back and put my horse away. That was when the roof fell in. I was not going to go all the way to Richardson's ranch. They said my horse may play out. I wanted to borrow Chicken, Norman's grey saddle mare. No such luck. It was me they figured would play out.

The snow had stopped by the time I had my horse unsaddled. Norman and Oscar were at the windmill. They were going to pull eighty feet of pump rod and they did not need me around there at all. I felt like something that had not much value. I went to the house.

Thelma found me a Zane Grey book to read. I was nearly half way through it when Uncle David returned, and that was at supper time.

The work was done for the day. The horses were at the ranch, the well was working and the livestock were taken care of. It was time to sit and visit.

There were Norman and Margie Nicholes, the school teacher. I think that they were married that fall. And there were Thelma and Oscar who had come to help with the pump rods. They were married later that year or the next. Uncle David and I were the rest of the joking bunch. I did not suffer from the poor little kid syndrome that had clouded me all day.

In one lull of the conversation Uncle Dave remembered:

"It was in the spring of 1930. The Chinooks had come to the prairie land, away north east of Calgary, Alberta. A neighbor had rounded up his horses, all but one. In time he found the horse in a neighbour's corral. It was wearing that guy's brand."

Uncle David chuckled when he remembered that episode.

"There was a lot of jawing back and forth, and even the police said that it was the guy's horse with his brand, unless someone could prove otherwise. Our neighbor had just lost a horse. It was lucky that horses were not very costly at that time, but still who wants to have a horse stolen."

"In the fall I helped him trim and neuter his colts. We had just done a full brother to the one that had been stolen. I said instead of branding this colt, let's give him a secret mark."

"We took a new ten cent piece and filed three little notches in the edge of it. It got disinfected good in the Croline pail, and we slit the skin on the underside at the base of the colt's tail, and slid the dime in. It healed over in a few days so he was sent out on the prairie for the winter.

In the spring he was missing. Sure enough the colt was at that same guy's corral with a new brand. The police got involved, and there was a court case over the ownership of the colt.

It was more like a circus than a law court. The horse was tied to a telephone pole in front of the building where justice was to be carried out in this small Alberta town. The plaintiff (the neighbor that raised the colt) had the cop and the judge feel the dime under the bottom side of the horse's tail. The defendant would not even bother feeling for the dime. The plaintiff described the dime in detail.

The judge told the police to get the dime out.

There it was the 1930 dime with three little notches filed in the edge.

The fella that had branded the colt looked at the dime and said, "Well, I'll be a son of a gun. So that was where I lost that dime." Then he tried to drop it in his pocket.

It did not work, and he got free board as a guest of the Alberta Government for a year, and wore a prison uniform. He deserved more time in jail, but that year they had all of the free help they could use.

The New Nash Car

When Andrew Tonjum became engaged to Edna Muri, he rented out his farm land and took on the job of grain buyer for The Pioneer Grain Company at Hallonquist, Saskatchewan. The company was glad to get Andy as their man. It would mean that they would get most of the grain grown on the south slope of the Wiwa Creek Valley. He was a son-in-law of the largest Scandinavian family, and the rest of the Norskies should follow along to the Pioneer.

His farm land consisted of one square mile of farm land. It was inconvenient that the farm was in two parcels that were six miles apart.

In the autumn of 1940 there was not much grain to buy. It had been a dry summer and a very poor crop. The Tonjums said goodbye to the Pioneer and Hallonquist, and moved to Vanguard, a town twenty miles south, and nearer to the farm land.

For Andy it was like throwing the rabbit into the brier patch. He was back among his buddies of twenty years ago.

To insure farm prosperity, Mr. Tonjum had a John Deere tractor with a new engine, new six inch steel spade lugs, three forward speeds and nice green paint. A brand new John Deere disk tiller. There was a four wheeled rubber tired trailer to haul tractor fuel and grease pails. To complete the outfit, Steve Chissum was put on the tractor seat.

Steve was tall, raw boned and skinny. He had run the pool hall in Halllonquist for the last couple of years. It had provided a very meager living. Then, too, the law had advised him to stop bootlegging because the next time they investigated his business, they would not close their eyes to anything. Steve was only too glad to close up the pool room and drive a tractor.

Charlie McCallum lived along the road south towards Aneroid. Many times in the past he and Andy had had a friendly drink.

Charlie had a piece of land that joined Andy's west farm. There was a ten acre field of alfalfa on Andy's land right next to McCallum's. Charlie's land was higher and sandy. For three years the wind had been moving it's soil across the road. For three years Charlie had not put a machine on that field. He let the weeds grow and at last had a good cover of dry weed stems. He had planned on one more year of weeds as additional cover.

Andy and Steve took the tractor and tiller and worked up a good fire guard. Andy went to the southwest corner and lit a match to the old alfalfa stems to kill off any bugs. With a SWOOSH the alfalfa field was burned to black ash. At the last moment a tiny little whirl wind crossed the corner of Andy's field. It carried the fire to Charlie's field. In less than an hour, Charlie's field was as black as Andy's alfalfa. It was as bare and exposed and as nude as could be.

That was when Charlie came home from town. When he saw his precious weed cover converted to ash, he was very upset. Charlie was tall and thin with a long face and a delightful smile. It was odd that when he gnashed his teeth his lower jaw had a bulldog look.

Charlie stopped his car and came face to face with Andy and Steve. The guy that used to be his friend sure gave Andy the bulldog look and some swear words plus a lot of screaming. Oh, but it was noisy in the corner of that black field!

With the soil bare, the wind could blow it away, so Charlie had to seed it. A half mile square field of wheat.

Spring, summer and fall Andy avoided Charlie like a hen would watch out for a hawk.

On a Sunday afternoon in the late fall there was a knock on Tonjum's door. Irene was ten years old, and she answered the door.

"Dad, Mr. McCallum wants to see you."

Andy felt , 'Oh no, not again,' but went to face the music.

Charlie pointed to the sparkling new green 1940 Nash car parked at the curb.

"After that fire you set, I had to seed that field. That crop bought me this new car, and two bottles of Scotch."

He thrust an oblong square box into Andy's hands. "That one is yours."

No hard feelings; they were friends again.

Because Of A Nail

Because of a nail the shoe was lost. Because of the shoe the horse was lost. Because of the horse the warrior was lost and so on until everything was lost.

Ed Williams gave that a reverse spin, and gained what he wished. He was a young fellow just out of school with no work experience. The streets of London or the English country side had nothing to offer Edward.

Kaiser Bill over in Germany cleaned his rifle and polished up his sword and made nasty faces. King George did the same and said something like, 'Let's have a go at it.'

World War One was officially open and Ed found himself in a British Army uniform.

Learning to march and salute officers was a bore. Carrying the Lee Infield 303 was another matter without glamour . Ed had hopes of becoming more than an infantry soldier.

Private Williams and another young fellow also had sore feet and a late pass. They had no money to spend, and nothing exciting to do. At a street corner near a Pub, they came face to face with an officer that had lots of rank. The important man parked his motor cycle, accepted the salute and entered the drink place. Ed could tell by the badges that this guy was from the Armored Brigade. Opportunity knocked.

Private Williams took an ordinary common stick pin from under his collar. He inserted it in the spark plug wire and left the point close to the seat frame. Ed's plan was that when the officer sat down on the seat it would lower enough to touch the pin and short out the bike's electrical system. Now all he had to do was loiter not too far from the motor cycle.

In time the officer came out, straddled the bike, gave it a kick start and sat down to ride away. The motor stopped. He stood up, gave another push on the start pedal, sat down to go, and it stopped again. The same thing was repeated a half a dozen times. The be-ribboned gent was exasperated. Ed strolled over so innocent and offered his assistance.

"May I help you?" the young soldier asked.

"Are you acquainted with the inner workings of this confounded machine?"

"Yes, Sir. Some, Sir."

"I say take a go at it, if you will, Private."

"If you will go to the Pub for a pint of bitters, I will try to correct the machine's fault."

The officer went back inside. Ed removed the pin from the spark plug wire. The motor started and ran as it should. Ed rode the bike around the block and stopped. He started and circled the block again. On the sixth trip around the block the officer showed on the scene.

"It seems to be working very well," was Ed's assessment of the case.

Reaching for his wallet the officer asked, "What can I give you for your service, old chap."

That break of military convention was all that Ed could hope for. For an officer to call a private 'Old Chap' was too good to be true.

"Sir, I would like a transfer to where I could develop my mechanical ability to a greater degree."

"What is your regimental number, Private?"

Private Williams had that number on the tip of his tongue.

Next morning when Ed got off the parade square, he was notified to report to the Armored Brigade.

The army training made Ed into a very good mechanic. After the armistice he was welcomed into the work force of a British automobile factory. Two years of that and he and his bride sailed to Canada.

General Motors of Canada needed a man like Ed. For years he was employed by G. M. at Oshawa, Ontario.

In the mid thirties the shut down time came to retool the factory, for the new models. Some executive had a brain wave. Speed up the assembly line by ten percent was the plan. The next week it was speeded up fifty percent. There was no way that men could work that fast. The Union went out on strike. The company was pleased. They were going to shut down for two months anyway. Ed was not happy because he was above the union group but below the executives. He and his peers got no wages for two months. Ed was never one to live with his head in the clouds, but the indignity of having to live on savings because of the shabby treatment of the company did hurt.

"General Motors have a truck branch in Regina, Saskatchewan.

There is an opening for the same job that I have here."

Ed and Mrs. Williams talked this idea in and out. The outcome was that they came to Saskatchewan. Ed worked at the G.M. building on the north edge of Regina.

World War Two came along. Soon there were no more trucks being built in Regina. The plant was geared to war needs. Then came the Armistice and no more war equipment. The factory was closed, and no more trucks either. Since leaving school, this was the first day that Ed had no job.

That only lasted one day.

"Hello, Ed. This is J.B. Sangster calling. We need you at Mid West Motors. Are you available and interested?"

"Yes."

Jim McLean joined the Mid West staff in June of 1950. I landed a job there in August of that year. We were about the same age. Jim was ahead of me with experience. He had been a mechanic at Abernathy, Saskatchewan for a couple of years. I had been a part time John Deere mechanic for a while. At Mid West I was in the auto body department.

We never stopped to reason why, but Ed Williams seemed to be on our backs quite often. Looking back, maybe he was trying to shape us up army style. Mr. Williams, the shop superintendent, seemed to us country boys to be a rare person. With a small reason he would give us the dandiest bawling out we'd ever had. Moments later in all friendliness, he would be back to tell a funny story.

After a bawling out by Ed that fairly turned the air blue, Jim tapped his foot on the corner of his work bench and philosophized, "Because of a horse shoe nail, the war was lost, and because of a pin, we catch hell every so often."

Cowboy Electrical

There was a good sized crew building that barn. It was November, not the best time of year to be pouring cement or climbing on a frosty roof. There were six of us sitting around the stove in the bunkhouse. We hoped that the heat from the stove would melt the cold that had settled in our bones during the day.

Bernard Reeder remembered a cold winter of the past:

There were five of us working on this ranch along the boundary. There was very little riding to do. Teams and pitchforks were the day to day grind. You would harness a team of horses, hook on to a sleigh with a hay rack, drive to the stack yard, fork it full of hay, and then go and feed hungry cows. When that load was gone, you got another one and fed more hungry cows. As I said there were five of us and the foreman and his wife. They had two kids, a little pest four years old and a new baby girl.

The lady of the house came up with a scary thought.

" While I am out at the clothes line hanging dippers in a blizzard, I may freeze to death." To her husband, the foreman, she pointed the next line. "When I'm cold and gone you will only have five guys to cook for and two kids to look after."

The boss got on the phone to the hardware store in Val Marie.

"Have you an electric clothes dryer at the store?"

We only heard the one side of the conversation.

"How much do you want for it?"

The price must have been right.

"How far are the roads open?"

This was the dead of winter.

"Well, that is about twelve miles from here?"

There was more talk about delivering a clothes dryer.

"What time could you be there?"

The dryer could be brought within twelve miles of the ranch.

"O.K. you be there at ten o'clock."

The boss turned to us, " Well, you guys will have one team less tomorrow. I have to take a team and meet the truck at the corner west of the Butte. I'll have to leave at seven so I can be there to meet the truck."

The next day we fed cows like crazy so we would be around to unload and hook up the dryer. The boss got home in the afternoon. We grabbed the dryer and got it into the house. There had to be some jackknife type of wiring done inside the house to accommodate the new dryer. It was all unpacked, and the wiring job was on track, when we were called to eat. Right after supper we were back at it. Right then there was something to live for besides cows.

The dryer was hooked up but it would not work. The following day we got through feeding early.

All evening we figured all the things that could be wrong with the dryer. Maybe we had to have the air duct to the outside before it would run. We cut the hole on the inside wall. Then we were able to get an iron rod pounded though the outer wall. We cut the hole around the mess we had made with the rod. Then the machine was vented to the outside and it still would not run.

Our next plan was to take the dryer apart and look for problems. That took up the next night. We had a flashlight that was also a circuit tester. Every thing that we could test seemed O.K.

The boss's pesky kid with his tricycle was always in our way. We got to the point that we would have liked to dispose of the little jigger. We knew that the kid's folks would be against that plan. If there would have been someplace to take the little cuss to get him out of our way, he would have gone there just a hell-a- hooping.

We were stumped. What could the trouble be?

The boss called back to the store.

"That new dryer you sold me don't work."

We had known that for two days.

"All right, I'll get there with this piece of junk by noon tomorrow."

The boss was slowly getting riled over the dryer deal. That was when the little pest came tearing past on his tricycle. He ran into the dryer door and it shut with a bang. Then the dryer started to run as soon as the door was closed. When the door was opened, the dryer stopped. Close it and it ran.

His Mother grabbed the little guy and gave him a big hug.

"Mommy's little man fixed the dryer. I'm so proud of you."

The darn little pest got all the credit, and us guys that added house wiring, checked circuits and forgot to close the door got laughed at.

Nitro Jerry

Ivan and Marchie had been our neighbours in the winter visitors park in Arizona. Now it was summer and the countryside around their home in North Dakota was beautiful, lush and green. We had stopped at their house one day. They live at Stanton, the seat of Mercer County. The Missouri River and Lake Sakakawea form the northern boundary of the county.

Ivan Stiefel had been the Sheriff for nearly a quarter of a century. To be elected five times in a row, was a feat that no President could equal.

We sat at their dining room table, and visited over coffee cups. A mention of the past was why Ivan brought out a scrap book of newspaper clippings and papers related to his former job.

"Somewhere here, are two pages that a prisoner wrote. He asked for a typewriter and paper. It was a deposition stating that there was no reason for him being held in jail. He claimed that the Chevrolet car was not stolen, the dealer in Iowa had let him take it for a test drive, and he was still testing it in North Dakota. The judge asked him who had done the legal document, and Jerry said that he had done it himself."

"It is a remarkable testament, but I must disallow it," the Judge said.

Ivan said, "I saved the paper because Jerry was one of my favorite criminals."

The first time I met Jerry was after the safe had been blown at a Mercantile in the county to the west of us. The sheriff and the game warden happened to be traveling together in the sheriff's car. They got a radio message about the robbery, and to apprehend a guy in a black Oldsmobile. They were driving west on one of the county roads, when over a hill came a black Oldsmobile at a terrific speed. The sheriff and game warden turned and gave chase. There was not much hope of catching the guy. They followed Jerry to highway 200 that passes a couple of miles south of town. Two miles west of our turn off, the Olds motor cracked up, and coasted to a stop on the edge of the pavement. It had run out of oil. The driver was a mild mannered, friendly guy, and it was no problem to put him in the back seat of the sheriff's car. Running out of oil, now that was just Jerry's normal luck. All the years that I knew him, he always had about that much luck.

They decided to bring the Olds to my office. The game warden steered the Olds. The sheriff in his car would run into the back end of it. It was not a steady push, but calculated little rear end collisions that each boosted the Olds up the road. This was done many times to arrive in front of our county building. This method of moving the crippled Oldsmobile could have given the game warden a whiplash, to say nothing of a quick trip to Kingdom Come.

If the game warden had known how close he was to reaching his everlasting, he would have jumped out of the Olds, and run screaming for the protection of a big rock, after the first bump and shove from the sheriff's car. The jar could have activated the nitro, and we would not have found any trace of the game warden or the black car.

This Jerry guy was lodged in one of our cells, and charges were laid.

I checked over the black car, and in the trunk I found a nearly new set of burglar tools. On the back seat, there were sticks of dynamite and nitroglycerine wrapped in a Holiday Inn towel. I called the explosive man at the coal mine. He came and took the stuff. He was a little bit touchy about the nitro, but he took it. He said that they would use it at the mine. On the front seat I found three pillows, also from the Holiday Inn. Jerry was less than five feet tall. He needed the pillows to sit on while he drove. Jerry went to the penitentiary at Leavenworth, Kansas. The insurance company took care of the black Oldsmobile.

That was the end of that case, so I thought. Jerry seemed to like our part of the country. He was forever blowing up a safe in western North Dakota. Well, that is what he would do every time he got out of jail. To Jerry, that was just going to work. That was his job.

One time when he was being released, I had to go to the penitentiary at Leavenworth and bring him back here to face another one of his safe blowings. That trip was over a thousand miles long, and I suppose that I got to know Jerry better than any other person. Well, I had so many dealings with Jerry after that trip. He had switched from dynamite only, to Nitroglycerine for the bigger jobs. We changed his name from Jerry to Nitro.

Over the years he developed diabetes, so instead of Leavenworth, he was sent to a reformatory in Oklahoma. The judge felt that he could get better medical attention and counseling there.

One day a sheriff from down near the capital phoned about some business. At the end of our talk he said that he had just seen Jerry on the street. I told him he must be mistaken. Nitro still had a few months to serve in Oklahoma. He said, " Well, he is here today."

The next morning I had just picked up the mail, and was going to my car, when out of the Welfare Office came Jerry.

I said, "Hello, Jerry."

The little guy looked at me and said, "You must be mistaken. My name is Harry . Welfare just bought me these ham sandwiches and a gas voucher. I am working with L&D, up on the highway rebuilding project."

I went to the office and called L&D. They had never heard of the man. The car he was driving was stolen. I drove down past the Union Oil station. There was Nitro at the pump filling his tank. I drove past and swung my car across the street to block his passage. He stopped and got out.

"What's the trouble, sheriff? I will be late for work if you hold up traffic."

He was always so calm and unflustered.

"Nitro, you have a stolen car, and I am arresting you."

I took Nitro to the cell, and had my deputy drive the car from Iowa back to the office. That was when he asked for the typewriter and paper to write his deposition .

When I looked in the car, there were the customary burglar tools in the trunk. On the back seat were the customary Holiday Inn towels and on the front seat were the three pillows. He always seemed to deal, if you could call it dealing, with the Holiday Inn.

It was just plain luck that I went for the mail and saw Jerry coming out of the welfare office, and he needed gas for the car. That gave me time to check him out. Goodness knows where there would have been a burglary and an explosion, if he would have been a couple of minutes earlier or later.

"Jerry, what have you got in the towels in the car?" I asked him.

"Pure Nitro." was his answer. "Be careful, sheriff. I have it wired to a control panel. Your radio could set that off."

I called the air base at Minot, and had them send help. In the meantime there was the Iowa Chev sitting on the street with all the Pure Nitro inside. It was a problem. With all of that explosive power, part of our town could go up with a big bang. I very carefully drove the Chev around to the far edge of the courthouse parking lot. We locked it up and put a snow fence around it.

The next morning the air force help arrived. A General, a Colonel, and a Captain. Now this was high powered help.

The Air Force men did not rush in. They looked at all angles. They finally moved the nitro a mile out of town to a gravel pit. Then ran the electrical cable the mile out to set off the blast. There was an additional big hole at the gravel pit after the explosion. Boy! What a bang!

The airmen wanted to interview Jerry.

I said, "Sure, but don't let him know that you blew his stuff up."

Two hours later they came from their talk with Jerry. These officers were dumbfounded.

"That man's knowledge is far greater than ours. We have not one man on base that could do what he is capable of."

I went to see Jerry. "I see that you still have Holiday Inn towels."

"Oh yes, I always patronize Holiday Inn. That is where I got the pillows, too. I like them people."

"What will we do with the nitro in the car?" I asked.

"If you will let me go out to the car, I can take care of it in a second," Nitro said.

There was no way that I would let him within yards of the Chev.

Nitro told me, "There is enough power lying on the back seat of my car to remove the jail, the courthouse, and the rest of this part of town. All I would have to do is get my hands on your police radio for a second. It would blow us all to kingdom come. But, I won't do that, sheriff, because I like you."

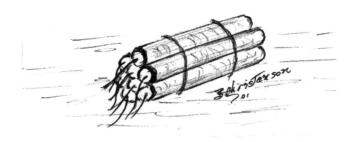

Mr. Graham

Did you ever pass up something that made you feel like butting your head against a brick wall? That time I sure was short as far as listening went.

We had been at Hodgeville that afternoon. Everyone from the municipality was there. The event that brought so many people to town that day was the Red Cross Mobile X-Ray Van. Everyone had to be x-rayed for tuberculosis.

Dick Graham was Knute Nybo's hired man. He was in his seventy-seventh year so it was really a case of free room and board. Knute and Stella had taken Dick and Miss Sutton, our school teacher, along for their x-rays.

Dick had a big thirst on. He was almost the first one through the van. He was also one of the first through the bar room door. Beer was sold at ten cents a glass. Dick did not fool around with dimes, he was more of a dollar man. Late in the afternoon when every one of the Nybo household was ready to go home, Dick was beer saturated. He was drunk.

About nine o'clock that night there was a heavy rain shower to the south. We were on the fringe of it, but still got a soaking. At eleven o'clock our phone rang. It was Stella Nybo.

"Can Bernie come and give us a hand. We have to take Dick to the doctor?"

Instead of using the car in the mud, I just ran the quarter of a mile across to the neighbors.

There was Dick sitting on a kitchen chair mumbling and moaning.

"In this mud we better have the thirty-five Chev. The new car has the vacuum shift and that will be too slow for these roads. I'll get it ready." With that Knute was gone

Dick sat without his shirt on. Stella had a firm hand on his left shoulder. His right shoulder point was low and forward of where it should be. That Dick was in pain was evident. His tears were caught by his mustache. He had two thoughts in mind.

"This arm is like an old dead tree its no good. Cut it off. Then hit me in the head and kill me. It hurts so much. Take the axe- - - - - - - -." His speech gave way to a pitiful moan.

Stella informed me, "He was going downstairs. He had to go outside."

Dick interrupted with a no nonsense voice, "I come, to her door," flipping his usable thumb towards Miss Sutton. "She said, GET OUT." Then I fell down stairs. I hurt my arm. Then I went outside."

He at least got rid of most of the beer that he was carrying. He then came back in the house.

To put on his shirt was out of the question. We did get his left arm in the shirt sleeve and let the rest of the garment slump. Next was Stella's largest tea towel. With it and some safety pins we made sort of a sling for the right arm. Then the shirt was draped over the injured arm and a couple of buttons were done up in front. All this went on to the serenade or roar. "It's dead, cut it off. Take the axe and hit me in the head," he kept repeating like a broken record.

The beer still dulled his mind , but seemed to have no effect on pain.

Knute was there with the 35 Chev. To get Dick in the back seat was as easy as loading pigs. It would have taken less time if we had been working with animals. Finally we were on our way. I sat with Dick and squeezed his right upper arm as hard as I could. I remembered when Uncle Sidney had cut out a sliver that had run in the length of my finger nail, Uncle David squeezed my arm until I had little feeling in my finger tips. I tried the same with Dick until he said that I was hurting him. I let go of his arm.

The first five miles of travel were not too bad, but then the road got real slippery. We were on a wet dirt road. Knute worked up a sweat keeping the car going south, it seemed to prefer going east or west. From Charlie Richards farm the road was dry. Knute made good time.

I had always been curious about this quiet old man. He had been in the community since before I was born, and I was now twenty-two. I was unmerciful when I questioned Dick about his past. In the last twelve miles to town I learned of his past.

Dick was born in Scotland. When a young man he joined the merchant marine. He jumped ship in Galveston, Texas. He soon moved on to Louisiana, where he got a job on the coal docks. The number of tons of coal each man had to shovel during the daylight hours was astounding. There he learned to drink beer. Every night the coal men would go to a tavern and drink quart after quart of dark beer. That was to replenish the body moisture that they had lost due to perspiration during the day. He made good wages and saved what he could. He became a trader. In 1900 he had two large warehouses at Corpus Christi, Texas. They each had a million dollars worth of trade goods from the Orient.

One morning his coachman was driving him home from the warehouses when the sea came in a big wave and washed them both away. Then a wave came in another bay and washed away his house, wife and two sons. That wave also took Dick's will to live.

Between answers to my questions, it was the same old cry, "It's dead. Get an axe- - - - ."

The Vanguard clinic was where Guy Seto has his store now. We stopped at the side door. Dick would not get out of the car. In 1935 Chev cars were made with the front doors opening to the front. All the doors were open and Dick got his left hand on the door post of the car. He would not budge. I was kneeling on the front seat trying to help. It was no use. I jumped out to go around behind him and shove. The door swung closed and pinched two of Dick's fingers. He let out a roar that brought Doctor on the run, still tucking his shirt in. When the door was open, Dick got out on his own accord. One glance at Dick and the Doctor directed us to the hospital. There Dick was given some kind of gas and he went to sleep. Doctor Hewitt snapped the shoulder joint back in place, and Dick woke up cold sober. It all took about a minute.

In the thin moonlight on the way home, Dick named every owner of each piece of land we drove by as if he were using a 1912 map.

Oh sure, I regret pinching his fingers.

This man had lived history, and I did not spend enough time with him. I should bang my head against the wall.

Free Help

It was sometime in the 1920's that the one legged barber walked into Chetik Lake Village. How far he had come on that wooden leg, we never did find out. Walking on two legs is bad enough but when one is made out of beaver food, it is so much harder. His pack was not much of a problem. All he had was a change of clothes and his barber tools. In those days even a tramp coming to the lake was big news.

Johnas got out his tobacco pouch and made a cigarette. It was a pleasant evening in June. We were sharing a pot of coffee at our picnic table.

The barber was at the end of his rope. He had no other place to go. When we found out that he owned a barber chair and a pool table things got interesting.

Dad had the sawmill at the lake and there were about twenty of us young bucks working for him. He would work the hell out of us all day long, but you know after a meal and a rest, we were as crazy as if we had not done a thing all day. There was nothing to do to kill time after work.

Some of the guys thought that they were pretty tough. There were a few black eyes and many many bruises. I don't remember of broken bones from their fights, but that pastime did not help the work at the mill. Dad gave me the hint of an idea. We would change these fighters into lovers. Well, they never did make the grade as lovers but they calmed down a lot.

We made a deal with the barber. If he could get his chair and pool table here, we would build him a poolroom and barbershop. BUT on Friday night we would move the pool table out of the way and have a dance.

Dad would furnish all of the lumber, the store would give us the nails and we would be away.

The barber wanted to keep strict records of the cost of material and labor. The materials were donated. Dad and the storekeeper figured it was a cheap way to give us young hellions something to do in the evenings. Boy, but we were building, as many as twenty guys some times. The barber with his notebook had every one's name down and the time he spent on the job. He made it clear that when he could afford it, he would pay everybody every cent that they had coming.. We did not want money. We wanted something to do. The poor fella had trouble when he wanted the name of someone working on the roof. He could not climb our homemade ladders.

At the time we were building, he was among strangers. Every time he would come with his book, we would give him a different name. We thought that it was fun to mix up the records for him. He had well over a hundred different people working on the building according to his records.

It was not a great building. It lacked a lot of things, like a foundation and square walls, but we had saws that would cut at a slight angle. As far as Dad and the storekeeper were concerned, the building had already served its purpose and the most fun of all was bugging the one legged barber about his account book.

We made the pool room and we had dances.

When winter came, Dad sent me out buying fur. That was the last that I lived at the lake. I don't know what ever became of the pool room or the barber.

Uncle Chet

When you are in an argument, and you know that you are right, why give up? Uncle Chet didn't. The three guys in a down town tavern in Minneapolis did not give up either. They just let on that they gave in.

When Chet left the barroom, he was not looking for trouble. He wasn't looking for anything, possibly, he could not see past his nose. The three fellas that he won the argument with took him behind the building and settled it their way. Early in the morning a patrol man walking his beat and checking rear doors came across a drunk lying there. Rolling the body to see the face, he decided that this was a prime candidate for the hospital. Chet was there for weeks.

Aunt Polly brought Uncle Chet along with her to Canada. Ben and Min Fritz brought them out to Grandpa Doll's farm with their new 1958 White and Pink Chevrolet car. Everyone was so glad to see the visiting relatives, with a hug and 'Come In,' they all went into the house. All but Chet, who was left standing out in the yard.

"Is this your first time in Canada?" I asked him.

He held up an arm and with two fingers out like he was ordering a couple of drinks at the tavern, he indicated that this was his second time in Canada. With a grunt he waved an arm, making a sweep from north east to north west. He mumbled, "Over there" was all that I understood.

Chet and I went into the house. Later I asked Aunt Polly what was the matter with Chet.

"Oh, he was out doing his tom cat prowl when someone beat him up. He never will recover," that answer alone gave his history and told of the burden she had.

It was a couple of years later we were in Minneapolis. At Aunt Polly's and Uncle Chet's apartment. He took my arm and sat me on the couch. He tottered to the hall closet and returned with an old photo album. It was a great effort for him to turn the pages. The first few were of hunting pictures taken in Minnesota. These he passed by. When he found the one of the Canadian flag at a Hudson Bay Trading Post he became excited. With much jabbing and mumbling he directed me to the trail he trod more than twenty years before.

Six friends got in a car and drove as far north in Ontario as there were roads. After a week of moose hunting it was time to return home. Not for Chet. His job at the tire shop was not calling that awful loud.

Chet bummed a ride on a small plane from Ft. Albany to Chesterfield Inlet. From there he shared paddling with an Eskimo in that man's canoe. They paddled past Baker Lake and on into the heart of the desolate North Land. Winter ice ended the canoe travel. The lucky cuss hitch-hiked with an Indian and his dog team. A plane ride to Fairbanks, Alaska and there Uncle Chet became a railroad bum and road the freight train to Anchorage. From there he gave up begging rides. The 30-30 Winchester had been traded for food, so he joined the United States Air Force.

When Chet waved his arm to the north that evening at Grandpa Doll's I thought he was shook up. When he showed me that photo album I thought he was crazy. But no, he was just that kind of a man.

Uncle Chet passed on and I was willed his treasured album, not in legal terms but in sign language. It had been his last tie with the past that he could partly remember, but could not speak of. On a page near the back of the album there is a bill of fare -

Nicollet House Thursday August 16 1860

The menu was somewhat different than that of todays. Of the things we cannot get today, are different parts off a buffalo, Prairie Chicken in Onion Sauce, Giblet Pie, and Succatash. Turnips were a big thing.

Oh yes, by paddle wheeler from Minneapolis it was 2000 miles to New Orleans.

Horse Sale

Mike and Punch Bitango lived with their parents east of Lethbridge, Alberta. Like any farm kids they would like to have been cowboys. They did have a horse, to them a wonderful horse. This animal was not just like the horse you would see at Canyon Meadows race track, but he was their horse and they loved him.

Whenever they traveled, they rode double. It would have been nicer if they each had a horse. Their dad Mat told them, "You can't have everything you want. It will take time and it will come to you."

One summer day a horse did stray into their yard. The boys put him in a corral. He appeared to be a real nice horse. Not as good as theirs, but still pretty good.

This strange horse that did not have a name had been there for several weeks. The brothers spent many hours currying and petting the stranger. They also discussed a name for him if he was their horse.

On their father's advice, they climbed on their horse and went to visit the local pound keeper.

"We have a stray horse at our place."

"How long has he been there?"

Mike said that it was after school was out for the summer. Punch agreed but added other local happenings. With the help of the pound keeper the time was established as five weeks.

"You boys bring the horse over here next Wednesday at 2 o'clock. We will have a pound sale, under the Stray Animal Act. Bring your money and whatever you bid will be the price you have to pay for the horse. You could put a thirty-five dollar charge for his feed at your place, but you would have to pay that with the price of the horse and in time you would get it back. It will save paper work if you don't bother with the charges.

All was set for Wednesday.

The great day arrived. Right after the noon meal, these two gaffers climbed on their horse. Riding bareback, Mike in front with the reins, meant that he was the pilot. Punch was riding behind and leading the nameless one to the pound sale.

Johnny a distant neighbor met the boys.

"Where are you guys going?"

"Oh, we are taking this horse to the pound sale. We are going to buy him."

"How much are you going to pay for the horse?" Johnny asked.

"We are going to pay eighteen dollars for him."

"Take care boys." Johnny drove away.

At the pound keeper's farm the boys had to wait until two o'clock.

The pound keeper was all set, and the sale was about to take place.

Johnny drove in and leaned against the fence as an innocent bystander.

"All right, gentlemen, according to the provincial stray animal act I will sell this horse. What am I offered?"

Johnny pipes up, "Twenty dollars."

He got the horse.

The kids rode home double on their horse, and hated Johnny for the rest of his miserable life.

Hunting

Raymond and Doris Fee farmed in the Twin Bay district. That was a few miles south west of Leoville, Saskatchewan. On that fall day a long time ago, Mrs. Fee knew that her oldest son Ted was grown up. As far as that goes, the twins, Albert and Art were considered grown up, too.

Albert drove his pick-up truck to French's yard.

"John, let's go hunting."

That idea appealed to John. "Sure, what are we going after?"

Albert replied, "Anything, Deer, Moose, Squirrels, Ducks, Chicken or what ever we find."

"For that kind of hunting we will need a Shot gun, the 30-30 and a 22." John answered.

"Yes, that is what I have. Get yours and we'll go." Albert was ready.

The hunters spent most of the afternoon stalking through the bush and every pot hole that may have a swimming duck was visited. In all of their travels they had seen neither fur nor feather.

The day's hunt was a complete failure. Albert had another idea.

"Let's stop at the farm and have a coffee with Mom and Dad."

At the farm Doris had hung white sheets out on the clothesline. There was no vegetation near the line, like grass or any clean growing thing. Just plain old dirt.

John and Albert stepped out of the truck. Ray was right there to congratulate the boys. As it turned out there was nothing to congratulate them for. They had not brought home a shred of meat of any kind.

John eying a clothes pin idly hanging on the line, took aim with his .22 caliber rifle .

"Watch that clothes pin. I'll make it spin like a propeller."

BANG, but the clothes pin did not spin at all. It went to the ground with the rest of the clothesline that got cut off by the shot meant for the clothes pin. There were the freshly hand washed sheets lying in the plain old dirt.

Raymond and his son Albert were rolling on the ground in unholy laughter. Mrs. Fee looked at poor innocent John still holding his rifle. Her eye had a cactus sharp look. Neither she nor John smiled.

Watching the Frogs Spit

She was a very pretty girl. Well, maybe very is too strong a word to use to describe her. At sixteen years she was not a ravishing beauty. She was a good looking, strong healthy girl.

There had come three things into her life.

First was Gordon. He was that dream boat guy that had just moved to town with his family. At first sight he appeared self-centered, loud, forward and many other adjectives that were added by the school girls.

The second thing was the parental permission to go to the Saturday night dance in the new town hall. Gordon had taken her to the dance two weeks in a row. In her mind all of the uncomplimentary names were changed to dream boat.

The third big change was the new telephone. Yes, the brown wooden box with the black pieces here and there. It was your entry to the party line. The telephone was the devastation of her happy dreams on this Saturday night. Listening in on the party line that afternoon she heard.......!

"Gordie is taking Jenny to the dance to-night. Won't that make someone turn green."

It was a rare autumn night. The sunset glow was still in the west. The full round silver moon had risen in the east.

She sat on a large sun warmed rock, staring at the water in the little creek. Hearing her father approaching, she held up one hand to signal caution.

In a whisper he asked, "What is the trouble Princess?"

"See that bull frog at the edge of the water. I am going to teach him to spit at GORDON!

With charm, beauty and sophistication, she has now retired as Fashion Editor of a large eastern daily news paper.

Mother Tongue

Paul, our next door neighbor, with his family had to leave their home in Austria with one horse hitched to a cart that held all of their possessions. They avoided the shells of the opposing armies. This is not a story of the heart breaking loss of their home and nearly every bit of their worldly goods. I think of the struggle they had with the language when they got to Canada.

Paul rode to work with me. German was his mother tongue. He was a wonderful rotund old man. Language was the problem. The only words I knew were Dumpf Kopft. That was what my mother-in-law used to call me with a laugh.

One time Paul got left thirty blocks from where he wanted to be. Other situations that did arise were usually hilarious.

Simon Harris and I made a deal on some eighteen foot Tamarack logs. Before coming to the ranch I had wore out two small old tractors by using them daily in the cold weather. I needed heavy poles to make a bale feeder. I would not require a tractor all winter long.

He was to cut them, and I would drag them home. His mother tongue was Cree. Simon cut the logs into six foot lengths. Eighteen feet was too heavy to lift. They were no good to me.

Misunderstandings by the million must have occurred around the world because of language differences.

Take Romulus and Remus for instance. The story is that they were brought up by a wolf. Naturally their mother tongue would be Wolf. When they decided to change those seven hills into the city of Rome, it must have been one great big shalalabaloo.

The contractor likely had the blueprints for the Colosseum drawn out on his slate. You know, just the small scale slate to use at the job site. Romulus could see a problem about the lion cage and also the gate to send the Christians in. Well, the contractor spoke Italian and the boys only spoke Wolf. The portly little man with the slate was proud of his plan. He waved his arms and the slate, and shouted out a lot of words in his mother tongue. He had to readjust his togo a few times. Romulus did not quite understand what the man was upset about. He barked and growled and pawed the air and carried on his side of the argument in his mother tongue.

Then it was Remus's turn to change some plans. Sure there was a box seat for the Emperor, but what about a place in the bleachers for their foster mother and the rest of the Wolf aunts and uncles. The shouts and screams in Italian mixed with the wolf howls must have gone on for months during the building of the early sports complex.

That discussion would be much worse than myself leaving poor old Paul thirty blocks from where he wanted to be, to say nothing about the six foot tamarack logs.

Simply Beautiful

It was in Old Yuma. Those three blocks were paved with tile and the street itself with its permanent stage or band stand in the middle of what used to be an intersection was in sharp contrast to the grand old buildings that lined each side. At one point there were benches that had a gracious bit of shade from a green tree whose name I did not know. I did know that a tree like that did not grow back home.

This was a mixture of religious holiday and craft market.

My legs started to ache from walking, so we sat down in the shade. It was only a minute or two until another couple wanted shade and rest. They were quietly asking one another about the parade. It seemed that they had more questions than answers. He finally turned to me.

"Do you know when the parade will start?"

"I just found out that it will be about an hour and a half from now," I answered.

"We will have a long wait," his wife observed, and then she added, "And where will it be?"

"It will start at the 'Sanches House'. You know, the oldest house in the city where they have the great little museum . It will come down the street over one block west and come over and into this street and end at the big round stage."

"Where did you learn all of this?" she asked again.

"We went to church early this morning and heard a short announcement there. We came early to get a parking spot close in so I would not have to walk very far. Then a guy setting up his stuff in one of the umbrella covered stands filled me in on the details of the parade."

I have heard that in Mexico in one province or another there is a religious holiday and a parade every day of the year. The Hispanic people of Yuma, Arizona are great for carrying on that tradition.

I added what I had learned. "There are two priests that are at some church function and it won't be over til after ten o'clock, so the parade will be late in getting here."

We settled into a friendly visit. They were from Oregon and we were from Saskatchewan.

Berniece said that she was going to the tee shirt booth to have a look.

We talked about the past in our respective lands. At one point Mr. from Oregon said,

"Things were plenty tough in our neck of the woods, nobody had money and everyone had debits. We scraped together enough to get a five dollar bill. When someone got the fiver, he would pay off a debt to another person. That guy would pay someone else. The five dollar bill circulated all over town and the countryside. Our economy was strong and everybody was happy. Then one day some darn fool took the five dollar bill and spent it. We were broke flat, every person was desperate, we had no money"

He said to his wife, "I'm going to look at the leather goods counter. Just wait for me."

"That was a sure enough case of poverty your husband mentioned."

"Oh, Joe can come up with some good ones some times. I prefer the true one's myself." She thought for a little bit and added, "People can be poor, just about any place people live."

The Oregon lady thought for a moment.

"There are many ways a person can be poor, and many ways to be rich, too."

"Years ago, there was a family that were next to facing starvation in Nebraska. Somehow they got to Oregon. The father could not find work of any kind. They moved into a deserted cabin on a mountain side. Someone gave the children a couple of orphaned lambs. Oh, those people were poor, but with skimping and saving they built up a large flock of sheep."

There were a daughter and son in the family. In Nebraska as a little girl she tripped and fell on a garden hoe. She got the most terrible cut on her face from her eyebrow to her chin. Of course, there was no doctor available, and in the end she had the ugliest scar. It pulled and twisted her cheek on her right side. Looking at her from the other side she was beautiful, but she felt that the scar had ruined her life for ever.

A young fellow from our neighborhood and one of his father's men rode past the sheep place one day. There was this girl hoeing in the garden. Maybe they really were thirsty. Anyway they stopped and asked this young Venus De Milo if they could have a drink at the well. She practically had her back to them when she said, "Yes, help yourselves."

Robert had never heard a voice as rich as hers.

It was a thirty mile ride one way for Rob, but a few weeks later he made the round trip on a Sunday. He got to know the family. He got to know them well and he should have because he was on the trail for two years. It took him that long to convince Emily that she had much to offer to a marriage.

They have been married for forty some years. Their daughter looked just like her mother but without the scar. She's had dozens of proposals.

I don't know if Rob has noticed Emily's scar yet or not.

Mr. Starblanket

We were living on the Spruce Creek Ranch. Berniece was working at the Leoville Hospital. She drove in to work every day. I foraged for myself at noon. I'll tell you the grazing was rather poor for me. I usually made a sandwich.

The lease fees were growing a lot faster than our cow herd. So I built a shop and did a bit of auto body and painting at the ranch. There was also a bit of buying and selling trucks. These were way down near the super economy range of vehicles, in other terms high quality junk.

It was a nice autumn day. I was working in the shop with the big door open. It was quiet and peaceful, just me and the dog. Three o'clock that afternoon the peace was certainly disturbed. First, by a Ford truck coming down the lane with a broken exhaust manifold. Secondly, by our dog Rowdy that seemed to dislike Indians. White guys' dogs don't like Indians and Indian dogs don't like white folks. I know! Isaac Chemakee's dog bit me on three different occasions, and it hurt each time.

I got the dog by the scuff of his neck and held him while a square faced smiling Indian approached, followed by his chocolate brown, red headed wife.

"Hi, I am Cedric Starblanket from Sandy Lake," he introduced himself.

Sandy Lake is the name of a reserve about fifty miles southeast of Spruce Creek.

"I am Bernie Christenson." We shook hands. The lady with the red hair was not introduced.

Mr. Starblanket announced, "I need a truck."

"Well, here is a Ford three quarter ton in very nice shape for eighteen hundred. And this is a sixty-nine Chev. I need nine hundred for it. Here is a sixty-seven Ford for four hundred, and it will run.

The three quarter ton was a nice looking truck. The Chev was one that I bought from R&R Motors in Vanguard, Sk. Wilfred Berg had bought the truck new. When he traded it in, I was right there to grab it. Well, really I phoned to Rob Puckett and made the three hundred mile trip to buy the truck. I had worked for Wilfred and I knew that his truck had not been abused. It served us well until we had to replace the differential with a used one. It was the wrong gear ratio and did that thing use gas. It did have the power of a locomotive. The other cheap truck was just cheap.

"Could I start the brown and white truck for you?" I asked. "It is only four hundred dollars."

"No, I like this green Chev truck. I have a boat and twenty- five horse motor and trailer that I would trade for the green truck. Next time you go to Prince Albert, stop in and see my outfit. Then we will trade. The boat the way it sits cost me twenty-four hundred bucks."

"Well, I won't be able to trade on a boat that good. You will need too much to boot."

"Oh no, I'll trade straight across," Cedric offered.

They left with my promise to see them the next time that I went to P.A.

It was two days later when I had just manufactured some baloney and relish sandwiches and the coffee had come to a boil. The peace was shattered again.

Our road across the hay field was just over a half a mile from the main road. The dog knew when this line was crossed. This day he just went nuts with his barking. I could hear the sound of a truck with a broken exhaust that had a drum beat accompaniment. Every second there would be a boom to go along with the eight cylinder growl. Here came Cedric with his red headed wife in their blue and white Ford. Bouncing along behind was a red boat on a home made trailer.

I had to leave my lunch and go and talk to the dog, and then greet the Starblankets.

"Hello, Cedric."

"Hello yourself. Here is my fishing outfit. The boat, motor, trailer and life jackets. The whole works, I'll trade for the Chev truck."

I looked the trade goods over. The boat was made of plywood. It had a very interesting shape, but the factory or makers plate was missing. The windshield was good, the steering wheel was not chewed up or weather-beaten, and the red paint was nice and shiny. In the boat lay the twenty-five horse power Evenrude motor. It looked like it had been used for a long time. The trailer had Ford wheels that were in use before 1950. In the boat were five life jackets. These things were more of a tie on float support rather than a jacket. They were red.

I thought to myself, 'To replace the life jackets would cost about the same as the truck is really worth,'

"OK, you got a deal."

I backed the boat into a corner of the trees, tied a tarp over it and ignored it for the next year.

One bright spring day I uncovered the Evenrude and took it to an outboard handy man at Chitek Lake. A few days later I picked up the motor with the report that it was in very good shape.

The boat had to be taken off the trailer so the tie down loops could be improved. I thought that to have it bouncing on the trailer like Starblanket had it tied, was not the best thing for it. The welding was finished and it was time to reload the boat.

Up until then my conscience had been slightly edgy about skinning Cedric on the deal. When I was winching the boat onto the trailer, I had to stop cranking and move the back end of the boat so it would be straighter on the trailer. When I lifted the boat, Low and Behold. I could see green grass through the bottom of the boat. Sure as heck there was a hole where the wood was rotted away. On closer inspection it had a great big hole.

We bought a different boat and trailer and mounted Cedric's motor on it. The life preservers were still tucked neatly between the front and back seat. There were four tie ribbons on each one, or there should be four. There was only one tie on the first four. They were useless. The fifth one was still worse. It had no ties at all.

With new life jackets, a six pound anchor, new registration numbers for the boat and an ice cream pail for a baling bucket, we were all set and legal. We were fishing on Huard Lake with William and Patsy Goertzen. Their boat was about four hundred yards from us.

A freak wind blew in from the east. I reeled in my hook and line. Turning the boat into the wind, I gave it all the throttle there was. One spurt of power and the motor stopped. One adjusting screw and its body fell out of the carburetor and into the boat. No tools, so what to do? Turned it back in with my fingers the best I could and got the motor running again. It was slow and sluggish, and no adjustment seemed to help. I turned to head for the dock which was only two miles away.

"Should we go and tell William and Patsy that we are going in?" Berniece asked.

Just then there was a snap and the fiberglass panel on the windward side loosened at the top.

"It will be better to see William and Patsy on shore rather than in the bottom of the lake," was my idea.

The next wave that hit us put gallons of water over the cracked seam in the side of the boat. Berniece grabbed the plastic pail and started baling the water that was threatening to put us on the bottom. Wave, after wave, promised to sink us. In the two miles she must have thrown a few hundred gallons of water out. I sat in the back and nursed the motor along.

There was a terrific amount of stress that fell away when we stood on the dock.

Every time I returned from Prince Albert I would stop for gas at Simonar's Service. One time I was at the counter to pay Ed, and here was Cedric Starblanket.

Cedric said to Ed, "Here is Bernie, the guy that sold me a truck that broke down before we got home. The wife had to tow me the last twenty miles. The transmission blew up."

I said to Ed, "And here is Cedric that sold me a boat with a hole in the bottom."

Cedric put his hand on my shoulder and said, "And we are still friends."

That was a comforting hand and it is very nice to have a friend.

I Killed Knute's Weathervane

It happened on a cold dark night in February. I was old enough to know better. Come to think of it, when is a person old enough to know better? There can not be a certain day in a person's life when one reaches that stage of intelligence. If there is, at least I had not reached it that night.

It was a short walk. A quarter mile across the field to have supper with Knute and Stella. The Nybo's were our closest neighbours. After a giant size meal we sat around and visited. The menfolks soon had the fancy table with the scalloped top and legs cleared of its doilie, and a whist game was in progress. Knute, Uncle Albin, Gordon Erickson and I do not remember who the fourth player was.

Basil Nybo was there. He had ridden horse back to get Knute's .22 rifle. His Dad, Albert, was going to borrow the gun for a day or two.

I went with Basil to get his horse out of the barn for his ride home. I was carrying the rifle. It was a Browning pump gun. It was as neat a .22 as you would hope to find. There was the long tubular magazine under the barrel. It would hold fourteen shells at a loading. You could just slide the forward stock back and forth and shoot. This could be done so fast that it was time to reload again right away. Basil had a box of shells in his coat pocket, but there were a couple in the magazine of the rifle.

It was dark and cold, the sky looked black and the stars were white.

Basil suggested, "I bet that you can't shoot the horse up on the barn."

Knute had this huge hip roofed barn. Up on the peak were three lightning rods with their three white glass balls. Some where on that ridge was also a weathervane. It was a prancing horse. Our plan was to hear the bullet sing as it glanced off the metal horse, if I could hit it.

One star was a bit brighter than the others around it. I maneuvered around until the star was hidden behind the horse. It was a simple matter to stand still and sight the rifle at the star, then lower the aim just a little bit and shoot. I did. There was no ringing glance of the bullet. Instead there was a thump, thump, thump, going down the other side of the barn roof.

Basil was the first to recover the power of speech. "You just killed a turkey."

We hurried around to the other side. Basil had his uncle's flashlight that I was to return to the house. There between the barn wall and a snowbank was the weathervane, lying flat and dead.

The horse was two plates of copper tooling soldered together to make the horse. It was mounted on a quarter inch cast iron rod. It was that little thin iron rod that I hit to bring the horse down to earth.

Basil got his horse out and mounted up. He handed me the flashligh. I handed him the rifle. He was glad to be on his way home. I was not glad to return the flashlight. I would have much rather had a tooth pulled than go into the house and admit to my crime.

Knute forgave me. I suppose that I should, too, but after sixty- three years I still feel that it was a dumb thing to have done.

Dexter

I was thirteen years old that fall. Neither Uncle Sidney nor Uncle Rienhart were able to ride. That nearly amounted to a problem for them. Dexter had to be taken home, and his home was forty miles north.

Dexter was an iron grey Percheron stallion about ten years old. He weighed more than three quarters of a ton. I did not like the big dumb nut. He did have four legs and an empty head fastened on the front end of his body. Uncle Rienhart had made a deal with his brother-in-law Norman Nelson for the service of this horse for the summer.

I feel that fate had been mean to Dexter, his parents had been wonderful animals. His offspring were good too, but poor Dexter in the middle of the family line, did not have much to recommend him as a horse show contestant.

It was in October that I got the offer.

"Will you ride Dexter home and bring back the colts from the river?" Uncle Rienhart asked.

"Sure, when do I go?" was my answer.

"You can take Dexter on Saturday morning. Then on Monday you can bring the young horses home."

Now that was good luck. I would be free of school for one day at least. Taking the big stallion was not so bright a prospect, but coming home I would have Uncle David's old saddle horse Snakes. He was big, agile and smart, and a dream to ride. Riding Snakes I would be able to bring the seventeen young horses home.

Saturday morning I was at Uncle Rienhart's bright and early. We got Dexter saddled and set for the road. His own bridle had a straight team bit. I crawled on. After many circles around the barn yard we were away. The horse was not enthused about going anywhere. We did get more than a half a mile away when the grey brute turned and galloped back to the barn. It was not a thrill to be bouncing along on a near ton of horse that was going his way but not mine. We stopped in front of the barn. Uncle came out. He had that metal eye shield with the white cotton padding showing around the edge, covering one eye. He was not happy to see us.

Dexter got a big surprise. We adjusted my bridle to fit the big horse. It had a curved bit.

I had my spurs tied on a saddle string.

"Are those useable spurs or just for show?"

"They are my new spurs," I answered.

"Well, get down and buckle them on tight."

That is what I did.

"Now get on and sit deep in the saddle. Then when he don't mind you rake him good."

He meant that I should scrape my spurs from the horse's shoulders to as far back as I could reach.

"If that don't work, jab him a few times." That was supposed to be enough advice to carry us for forty miles.

The next five miles were a learning experience for both of us. We were jogging along and I was about ready to give out with a Wilf Carter cowboy song, when Dexter darn near jumped out from under me. Then we thundered down the road on a dead run. At last I got him stopped. There back on the road was Clarence Paulson standing with his bicycle.

"I am sorry that I scared your horse," he called.

"That is all right. Come on up," I said.

Clarence rode beside us for part of a mile. We had a great visit. We came to Paulson's driveway, Clarence turned in. Dexter turned as well, and we had another set to. It seemed that the big grey horse had formed a romantic attachment to the bicycle.

Some time after three o'clock, I crossed the railroad tracks at Herbert. It was only a block to the livery barn. There was no one around so I put Dexter in a stall and loosened the cinch. He had some good hay to fill up on. I was gant, too, so it was over to Wan Gin's for a pork chop .

Back at the barn I put the bridle back on instead of doing it at the water trough when the horse finished drinking. If he would have gotten away from me I knew that I would look dumb if I walked along behind the horse carrying the bridle.

While the horse was drinking, Bob Doaks, the fella that owned the barn, and another man came from over town.

"I had this horse tied in your barn while I was over having a bite to eat. How much do I owe you?"

"Did you grain him?"

"No, he was too warm for that," I answered.

"That is all right. Then it is nothing," Mr. Doaks said. Then added, "That is a pretty big horse for a kid like you to handle."

Just then Dexter gave out with a whiner that echoed back from the hills. I gave him a tough boot to his belly, and he paid attention. The kid part of Mr. Doak's observation kind of rankled me.

"This horse has gotten a lot smarter since he met me this morning." Boy was I ever big and brave. I mounted up and rode north out of Herbert.

We traveled on across the big slough with the cat tails, passed the Frances' farm and on into the rolling land towards Gouldtown. My horse seemed to get the lay of the land. He could tell that home was just on the other side of a few more hills. He became easy to get along with.

We came to a small valley, and the horse of his own accord broke into a gallop. We were making good time for a change. From the hill on the other side came a car with its lights on. It was still not very dark. It was Norman and Marjie and Oscar and Thelma in the rumble seat of the model A Ford Roadster. Norman had come to a stop with the car. I stopped beside them.

"You are riding that horse rather hard, aren't you?" Norman asked.

"Oh, we have walked most of the way from Herbert. In fact most of the way from Uncle Rienharts. And now Dexter just wanted to run." I said truthfully. The walked part was a lie.

Norman had been around horses long enough that he knew that a horse does not lose his hay belly by walking forty miles.

"You have just a few miles to go. Put him in the barn. Ma is home she will feed you. We are going to Swift Current to a movie."

The feeling of doubt about handling this big clown of a horse was fading away. He was soon at his own home.

Aunt Olina gave me supper, and visited while I ate.

"Couldn't R. J. find someone older than you to bring that horse home?" She was some what miffed at her son-in-law's choice of horsemen.

"No," I answered. I thought that I had done pretty good, but everyone else seemed to think that I was a little kid.

Uncle Rienhart and Aunt Nora were at Nelsons the next forenoon. I was in the barn currying and brushing Snakes for the ride home tomorrow. I felt let down. Norman and Oscar had brought the colts from the river earlier in the week. That meant that I lost out on the best part of the ride. From the other section of the barn I heard voices.

Norman said, "I sure don't like the way that kid made all of those spur marks on my horse."

Here I had brought the big dumb horse home and got criticized for doing it. That was a blow.

"Well, you are darn lucky I wasn't riding him, or he would have had spur marks from his ears to his tail," Uncle answered.

Boy Oh Boy! That made me feel good.

Bachelor

The weather had been hot and dry. The weeds were tall and green and sucking the moisture out of the ground. Clarence had to kill those weeds, they were endangering the next year's crop. The field was big. Round after round he drove his tractor pulling the discer. After a pass with the machine the soil was left clean and brown, and the weeds were gone. A small start was made one afternoon. The second day was long, hot and tiring. The tractor had no cab so Clarence was at the mercy of the summer sun and it was hot. The third day saw a finish of the job. It was near noon when Clarence parked his tractor.

The bachelor found himself a scanty lunch. He took stock of his grocery supply and decided that it was time to make a trip to the store.

The Chevy pick up truck purred along like a kitten. The truck seemed to cough going up the steeper hills. Clarence could tell that he would soon have to change the engine's spark plugs. He had thought of the spark plugs last week when he was fixing fence. The hammer and staples were still on the seat beside him as well as the small role of rusty barb wire and a few odd tools.

At the grocery store his food supply fit into a cardboard box. That he put on the floor on the passenger side of the cab. Then another thought struck him.

"Do you have any loaves of frozen dough?" he asked.

"Do you mean frozen bread loaves?"

"Yes, that is what I want," Clarence said. "That is a much better invention than sliced bread. I can bake this and slice it myself."

"Do you want two of them?"

"I would like twelve of them. They keep so good in the deep freezer. I can take one out and bake it whenever I want fresh bread." Clarence was sold on this new system of making bread.

The clerk asked Clarence, "Will it be all right if I put them in paper grocery bags?"

"Why sure. I can set them on the seat beside me. That will be good," Clarence assured her.

It was a hot day. Remembering the heat that he had endured for the last three days, he figured that he owed himself a cool beer. In the bar room were other men of the same disposition. The weather was soon talked out. There were only seven of his friends present.

"Hey, waiter, bring us another round," Clarence was buying.

"Heres to ya"!   "Skoal" and all of the other bar room thanks.

Then someone else bought a round.

"Did you hear the one about the farmer that had three ducks?" The story was told, and every one had a big laugh.

Someone else bought a round.

"Did you hear the one about the drunk riding the elephant down the street in the middle of the night?" It was told and some were left choking with laughter and slobbering in their beer.

Another round and later another one. These guys knew how to use up a hot day.

The cool of the evening had settled over the country side. It was time to go home.

Clarence had parked his truck facing into the sunshine. Now it was in the shade of the hotel.

"Oh my! Guys, look at my truck. There is no room for me in the cab. What can I do?"

Clarence was faced with a big white blob of something against his window. The twelve loaves had become unfrozen in the eight hours that Clarence had been in the hotel. It had risen and risen and kept right on rising.

"Clarence, you did not tell us you were going to make bread. You should have come out and kneaded them down once in a while."

The unholy shouts of laughter from his friends did not help the bread dough that had a hammer, barb wire and a lot of other things in it.

Apple Pie

In the beginning, Arling called, "Can you help us for a few days?" My answer, "Sure."

Arling and Woodrow Newton were at our farm in just a short while. The car's trunk lid was opened and I threw my saddle and chaps in on top of Woodrow's rigging. The cousins went to the door of the house and said Hi to Mom. The next stop was at Donald Burton's. Donald and Arling had the brain wave that with all of the surplus horses in the southwest a profit could be made. All they had to do was buy a herd of these horses, move them north and sell them to the lumbermen. Woodrow and I were on the first level. When the horses were found and bought, we would chase them somewhere. The destination was not our problem.

During the trip around the south country we got to Val Marie on Friday noon. The nuns had young students out beside the convent for some kind of a game.

Our aim was the hotel dining room. Woodrow and I left our hats on the shelf as Donald and Arling did with their caps. The dining room was a dignified looking place. It had many square tables with white linen table cloths and four chairs at each table.

The waitress that came to our table to take our order was a tall slim young lady and she was very attractive.

It started out as just being funny. Who would have thought possible the consequence, that would follow.

She did not get a chance to more than smile when Donald said, "Four pork chops, please."

I interrupted, "This is Friday, isn't it?"

Everyone agreed.

This was long ago and the Catholic Church at that time still had a rule against eating meat on Fridays.

"Could I have a halibut steak, please?" I meekly asked the girl.

With a very warm smile she assured me that I could.

In just a jiffy I had a large plate of food and the golden halibut was in the center. Donald, Arling and Woodrow sat and watched me fill my face on the fish dinner. It seemed to stir up their appetites, while I was wolfing down the halibut. I was almost finished with my plate before the three pork chops came.

That same pretty girl came and took my empty plate and asked, "Would you like a piece of apple pie?"

I smiled back and said , "Yes, please."

She set in front of me the largest piece of apple pie that I had ever seen in an eating establishment.

If it would have been a race, it would have been called a draw. When the guys were finished their pork chop, I was finished with my pie.

The waitress came and gave me a friendly smile again. She then asked if my three companions would care for apple pie. They were all in favor and all enthused. The enthusiasm melted away when they saw the size of their pieces of pie. Their three pieces put together were just a touch bigger than the one she had brought to me.

Donald paid the bill. Outside he did not wait until we were in the privacy of the car. He lit into me right on the sidewalk in front of the hotel.

"Why did you lead that girl on? Made her believe that you are Catholic. You should be ashamed of yourself, ordering halibut because it is Friday."

"But, Donald, I like halibut steak."

"Oh, Josh, you were just trying to make a hit with that pretty waitress." He was still peeved with me.

"I have never seen her before and I don't suppose that I will ever see her again. But I did learn one important fact."

"What was that?" Donald was still a wee bit upset with me.

"I learned that Catholic pieces of pie were much larger than for Protestants." I told him.

Donald gave a snort and sort of gave up on me.

P.S. Just a few years later I met a person that could have been a sister to the waitress. She was tall, slim and very pretty and with such an engaging smile. We fell in love. For fifty years she very often makes apple pie and serves me a Catholic sized piece. I still feel that she is pretty.

Changing Times

Wind and weather wear down mountains. That change does not effect our lives nearly as much as changes made by people themselves.

The Northwest Mounted Police made Regina, Saskatchewan the hub of their prairie district. It soon followed that there were so many items collected that a museum would be the way to display them. In the mid time of the last century, the museum was located in a basement room in the Police barracks. This was a reasonably large room. There was a wealth of material on display.

The variety of items gave an exciting look into the work of the force. So many small things added up to the success of our law enforcers. A person could get lost in western development and history for an afternoon, and wonder where the time went.

The RCMP museum was a place to take out of town visitors for a different few hours.

Thirty years later I had an occasion to go back to see the museum. It had suffered a gigantic change. It had moved upstairs. There were pieces of memorabilia in little curtained off alcoves. It would remind you of some social climbing lady that hosted a garden party and served tiny little baloney sandwiches. The good stuff must have been locked away in the basement. What a lousy change! It was, not the homey place of bygone days. It had gone high hat.

The modernization of the museum I could have done without.

The depression of the thirty's everyone could have done without. Johnny's father had a poor piece of stony ground close to Regina. The only way that he could provide for his family was to go to jail every fall. He would distill a gallon of home brew, and try to peddle it on the streets of the city. Every fall he was arrested and his moonshine equipment seized. The government would have to furnish coal and food for the family while the bread winner was in jail.

Johnny worked at the garage where his friend Red Henderson worked. I too was there stuck in a corner of no importance.

John Vandanbush was a smart looking man. His blue eyes and blond mustache were striking.

Red Henderson was about six foot four in his stocking feet, but no one ever saw him in his stocking feet. He always had a winning smile to go with his red hair.

Red's wife Nel had two of her aunts from Ontario visiting for a week. On Sunday afternoon Red and Nel and the Aunts were in the car to go and see the Police museum. At that moment John and his wife dressed in their Sunday best came to call on the Hendersons. Introductions were made and Vandenbushs joined the trip to the police barracks.

Mr. John K. Vandenbush with his tan trench coat and snap brim hat was noticed by the number of tourists in the museum. He had the appearance of a company director if not the chairman of the board.

In the basement room that was the museum in those days there was a collection of stills for the brewing of alcohol. Some were large and impressive, others were simple and poorly made. They were displayed along the south wall of the room. One thing they had in common. They had been confiscated by the police as tools for making illegal alcohol.

Red was with Nel's aunts on the far side of the room.

John waving an arm in the air called, "Red, Red come over here."

That call brought a flock of tourists ahead of Mr. Henderson. There was the executive looking Mr. Vandenbush pointing to a beat up old wash boiler that had pieces of pipe clumsily soldered into the cover. The pipe made a very crude bend.

"Red, that is the still the cops took away from my old man in 1931."

Feeding The Multitude

Paul and Mary Lou live in Oregon on a farm three or four miles from town. The farm is a twenty minute drive from the State Capital where Paul's business is located. Paul and Mary Lou are not active farmers. He is a retired Air Force Officer. Still retired as a young man, he bought into a local business with his brother. Mary Lou is a stay at home Grandma. Her summer days are filled with grandchildren, housekeeping, preserving and canning the fruit and vegetable that she grows in abundance.

The house that they have is something to behold. It is large. Many rooms and many levels. The kitchen is large enough to entertain in. The sauna is large enough for all of the grand children to be in at one time.

Paul is very active with the Knights Of Columbus. That is the church's men's club. Mary Lou is a good cook and active at that.

On a Wednesday morning a neighbor lady called.

"Mary Lou, you make such wonderful bread. Will you bake some buns for the big doo we are having at the K.C. hall on Saturday night?"

"Yes, I will be glad to help out."

Mary Lou did not question the reason for the buns or what the function was. Paul would know. The ladies chatted for a while. The weather, their gardens, local happenings were talked over. They had a good old phone visit.

"Oh, how many buns will you want?" Mary Lou asked.

"Six hundred would do just fine."

"OK Ruth, it's been nice talking to you."

Mary Lou hung up the phone and went to the kitchen.

"SIX HUNDRED BUNS. What have I gotten into?"

Wednesday night the bun count was about one hundred and fifty. Thursday's production was better. Friday was not quite so good. Four hundred and fifty buns. One hundred and fifty to go and one day to do it.

Mary Lou called two of her sisters, "Hi, Sis, could you bake fifty buns for me tomorrow morning? I will come and get them right after noon."

The second sister got the same message.

Both ladies had the same idea, "Oh, I can drop them off at your place tomorrow ."

Saturday evening, "Paul, I have to take buns to the Knights of Columbus hall. Why don't we get dressed up a bit and take them down."

Paul was agreeable, "What is going on at the hall tonight."

"I have no idea. I have been so busy baking buns that I have had no time to talk to anyone."

With their arms full of big boxes of buns, this couple was utterly surprised to step into the hall and there was a wall to wall banner with a very clear message.

HAPPY ANNIVERSARY, PAUL AND MARY LOU.

Cinders

Uncle Reinhart Muri was an old time horse man. He was born in Montana in 1893. He drove a team of horses and had the job as straw monkey on a steam thrashing outfit in 1900. By the time he turned out his last horse and threw away his work gloves, he had had years of horse experience .

When I was a little kid, he had four big Percheron mares: Bell, Daisy, Queen, and Judy . These four horses would weigh darn near as much as a steam engine. I, with all of my six year old knowledge was sure that they could pull as much as a steam engine. Uncle had more horses than these, but the gray mares were his favorites.

Big, gentle, faithful, tame, friendly, any nice adjective would describe these horses.

One of these mares was Cinder's mother or grandmother. He was gray but he was smaller by a few hundred pounds. He was not gentle, or tame or friendly. He was not mean, but just chuck full of mischief. When R.J. wanted horses in the barn, he would take a small pail of oats to the gate and call. They all came but Cinders. He would get close enough to taste the oats, then turn, put his tail up and gallop around the pasture for a few minutes. To Uncle R.J. this was not good horse manners. When Cinders was in harness, he was as good a horse as any of the others.

One spring day Cinders went for a stroll, and he took two other younger horses with him. They were seven miles from home when found. I was requested to go and bring them home. My saddle horse Peppermint had developed a bad case of kidney failure. I borrowed a horse from Basil Nybo.

His horse was Thoroughbred crossed with dynamite or some kind of explosive. I used her to bring Cinders and company home.

Things were going too good. We were galloping down the road. We came to the corner where highway 343 turns to the east. It was a dirt road at that time. Cinders planned a joke. He thought that he was the fastest running horse there was. He turned north, but I cut him off. He was disappointed. Just to show me he laid his ears back and ran away from me. He did not know that I was riding one of the fastest running horses in the country. I took out about six feet of lariat rope and rode beside Cinders. Every few yards I would smack him with the rope and give him a big Ya Hoo. This went on for three miles. I figured that I had better slow up. No sense in blowing the lungs out of a horse. Not Cinders, he would not give up or slow down, not until he was home. I had to wait a few minutes for the other two. Shortly, we were all home.

Jerry Myers, a rodeo stock contractor from Moose Jaw was married to Harriet Newton, a niece of RJ's. For a year or so Jerry would stop a study Cinders.

Years later I asked Uncle, "What even became of Cinders?"

"I loaded him in the one ton truck and took him to Jerry's in Moose Jaw. We had planned to train him to be a bucking horse. Have him ridden a couple of times, but have a buck off before he really got wound up. That way he would learn that he could unload a rider, and become a good bucking horse."

"Jerry told his man to jump off at about the third buck. Well, this guy got on and rode the daylight out of poor Cinders."

The poor horse just stood and trembled.

"Why didn't you buck off like I told you to?" Jerry asked his cowboy.

"What! And let an old plow horse buck me off. Do you think I'm crazy?"the proud guy answered.

"You are not only crazy, but you are fired. Your stupid ride just ruined a good bucking horse. You have got to be the ----------- ------- --------- ---------- --------- ---------- that I have ever seen. Get your things and get off the place right now."

R.J. said, "Jerry was mad and used language that was beyond me. It was good that Jerry cussed him out so I did not have to, but I felt like it."

Uncle looked at me and said, "You know there are countless ways to spoil a horse."

The Broom Truck

It was a cold day in January. Not the forty below zero Canadian prairie cold, but Kansas miserable cold. It was above freezing but the furious north wind that blew the heavy grey clouds across the sky was cold. That wind seemed to knife right through a person. It did not give one a good feeling to stand out by the gas pump while you filled your empty tank.

Berniece and I and her sister and friend from Minnesota were with us. We were on our way to Arizona.

They did not have a sunset that day. The clouds just got darker and then it was night. We stopped at Long Island, Kansas for the night. At the motel our registration was completed and the room key was in my hand. Three truckers with their tote bags had just entered the lobby.

To be friendly and out going I said, "This has been a cold windy day."

The most mature man of the group answered, "The worst day of my entire life. Since day light this morning we have made ninety miles down the road."

"Has the wind been that hard on your traveling?" I innocently asked.

"It sure has. Every time we changed a tire on the left side the wind on our back was trying to push us under the rig. When we replaced a tire on the right side, the wind came under the rig and sort of moved us away."

There was me again, "Did you have two flat tires."

"No, it was closer to fifty."

The guy between the big rig driver and the fellow signing in for the room turned.

"It was more like a hundred as I remember."

I was all sympathy, "Was it bad roads or bad tires that gave you the trouble?"

"It was a bad load that was the problem. We are moving a portable asphalt plant from Garden City, Kansas, to Missouri.

It is a hundred and ten feet long and weighs eighty-four tons. The weight is what is hard on our tires."

After a good sleep it was morning. We were packed up and went to the lobby for the included breakfast. There were the same three truck drivers.

"Good Morning, Gentlemen. It is a bright clear day out there," I greeted them

"Oh, it will be a great day for traveling," the long load man was cheerful.

"Where have you parked your trucks?" was my question.

"The big rig and the broom truck are out north six miles. We came in with the Escort Vehicle."

"What on earth is a broom truck?" That was a new one on me.

We were munching toast and sipping coffee at a round table right beside the truck men.

"The broom truck is really our pilot vehicle, except that it also has the broom."

"What do you need the broom for?" I didn't know.

"It is not a regular broom. It is a few plastic blades behind the cab. They are set some higher than our load. They are firm enough that the wind does not affect them. If we go through an underpass and the blades of the broom touch the overhead the load has to go through at five miles an hour and very carefully at that."

"There was a driver that missed his turn off. He went barreling through the underpass. He had lost his broom truck so he found a cross over and come tearing back to find his pilot. The other side of the underpass was ten inches lower than the side he had just went through. On the top of his load was a generator. It caught the support beam of the highway above. That rolled the generator on end, but it lifted that lane of the road about three feet. The weight of the road above crushed the generator down into the load below and the highway settled down again.

A fella in his new Ford economy size car could not believe his eyes when the road heaved up, but he was late for work and the road came down just in time for him to race over it."

This had been told by the big rig driver. His Broom Truck driver with a far away look said, "The broom truck should never be behind, but always in front of the load."

In our party there were Berniece, her sister Florence and her friend Dorothy and myself. When we got in the car, the idea of going six miles out of our way to see an asphalt plant and a broom truck was voted down three to one.

I suppose they put the broom truck out in front.

Law at Work

It had been a quiet night. The Sheriff's Deputy, Joel Diers, had cruised around town for most of the evening. There was no one that needed help. He thought, 'Crime must have gone to bed early.'

The car had the sign on the door that said Sheriff and under the big bold letters it also said Wright County in smaller letters.

Everything was as it should be that night. The athletic rippling muscles of the young man were all poised for something to do. But there was nothing.

Deputy Diers was checking a county road. A few miles out of town at the crest of a low hill he found a problem. The snow plow had left a ridge of hard packed snow on each edge of the narrow pavement. The windrow of snow was three feet high. At the top of the hill a half ton truck was sitting right on top of the snow ridge. It was a case of high centered and perfect balance. The truck sat with each wheel more than a foot above the road. The truck lights were on and the rear wheels slowly turning.

Joel shone the flashlight in the driver's window. The man was hunched over the steering wheel asleep.

"Open up in the name of the Law."

The fellow woke up. He sat very erect, shifted into drive and gave it a bit of gas. "The cop is standing beside my truck so to heck with him. I'll just drive away and leave him stand there." The driver was obviously drunk.

Deputy Diers started walking on the spot, swinging his shoulders in time with each step.

The driver glanced out the window and saw the law man walking beside him. It was easy to see that he would have to speed up to get away. The fact that he was still stuck did not penetrate his booze clouded brain. Stepping on the gas made the rear tires spin faster. The Deputy changed his gait to running on the spot.

The drunk looked out the window again and here was the lawman still running beside him. He snarled, gritted his teeth, hunched over the wheel and put his foot down. The back wheels were fairly whistling with speed. There was the darn policeman still running beside him. The driver leaned far forward over the wheel and stepped the gas to the floor. He was stuck, hadn't moved the truck one inch since he had woke up. Joel had the snow packed down with his running on the spot, but now he was running all out, going as fast as he could run so it must have seemed to the guy in the truck.

Joel stopped running. He opened the door, reached in, turned off the ignition and pulled the keys.

"I can not spend the night running beside your truck. Come with me. You will be a guest of the county tonight," Joel informed the driver.

The big burly drunk meekly went to jail thinking, 'I must have drove six to eight miles and he ran beside me all that way. How could he do it?'

The Electric Rabbit

I may as well start out with a bit of family history. Uncle David and his son Danny were here from Alberta for a visit. Ivan and Philip are brothers and nephews of Uncle David. I am another nephew.

It was at the Hallonquist Rodeo. The rodeo and community hall are about all that is left of Hallonquist, Saskatchewan. Oh, there still is a great community spirit.

For a road side rodeo it was good. The contestants, the stock contractor, the Town and Country Club, all together made it a great day.

The wind up for the day were the Gray Hound races. Philip had two of his dogs in the race. Ivan, Danny, Uncle David and myself, were in a little group, between the Para-Mutual tent and the race track. We were two dollar gamblers. Uncle did not fight the mob to place a bet on the dogs.

It was near the last of the races. Philip's dog was wearing the blue jacket, when they were paraded. I put a two dollar bet on the Blue.

Uncle David said, "Here, Ivan, go and put fifty dollars on Philip's dog."

There was some hesitation. We were two dollar betters. Here was an orange fifty dollar bill.

"Do you want to bet the whole works?"

"Why sure, go and get the ticket." Uncle was definite.

Over the sound system came the voice, "Betting window is closed."

Uncle returned the big bill to his wallet.

The Electric Rabbit just whistled across the arena. Philip's dog was right behind.

I took my ticket to the pay window and collected sixteen dollars.

Uncle David started to figure, "Sixteen on a two dollar bet. Fifty dollars would bring in, lets see, um? Aw heck, I knew that dog would win. You would think that rabbit had diamonds the way that dog of Philip's ran."

Just Color

When we were kids, cousin Joann and I met often. She grew up, and I had not seen her as a lady. Then she got married. We were pleased to meet her new husband, Allan, while they were on their honeymoon.

For years and years our paths did not cross. In that length of time many things happened to all of us. Joann and Allan were no exception.

Allan is a licensed plumber. His boss asked him to move to Nelson, B.C. and manage that branch. Allan moved to the new job.

It appeared that a housing developer had a big project in the works. For some reason or other, things had bogged down. Allan with calculated bravery made a deal on one of these houses. In a short while the project was going again full speed ahead.

Joann was staying at the old home, until the children were finished that school term.

Allan phoned, "Guess what, my Dear? I have bought a house."

"Did the dog come with it? If so, is there room for both of you to sleep in it?" Then Joann hung up. To herself she thought, 'With the amount of money we have to buy with, it would have to be a dog house.'

Joann helped out at a café during the rush hours.

Weeks passed by and one noon hour a gentleman with floor covering samples came into the café. He seated himself in the center of the dining room. Joann was carrying a food tray in a hurry.

"Pardon me, but are you, Joann Rasmussen?"

"Yes, that's me," and didn't even break stride. She just kept right on a going.

Joann scooted by with a heavy tray of food.

"I must get your choice of floor covering for your new house," the salesman stated.

On her return she stopped long enough to say, "So, you are in on the joke, too. Well just forget it." She was a busy girl right then, and had no time for Allan's tom foolery.

"Please, Mrs. Rasmussen, would you like a rug?"This guy was at the point of pleading for answers.

"That would be fine." And she was gone.

When she was passing the rug sample guy, he asked, "How about this one?"

As she ran by, "That will be good."

The salesman made a note on his order form.

"Where do you want the rug?"

Over her shoulder, "Door to door."

She ran by again, with another order of food.

"What color?"

Joann shouted back her answer, "Lemon yellow."

The rug merchant made the last note on his order blank, and went to a quieter café to get something to eat.

School was out, and the Rasmussen family joined Allan at Nelson. The new living accommodations were a surprise. A ranch style bungalow, just beautiful, even with out the landscaping completed.

Joann was impressed, but what really took her breath away when she opened the front door was Lemon Yellow rug. Yes, door to door.

Bert's Car

Bert Galant worked for Ben Newton. Bert was a good steady guy, a nice fellow to have around besides being a good worker.

It was on a Sunday morning in July, 1926.

"Say boss, I run into a good deal in Vanguard last night." Bert nearly glowed.

"What kind of a deal was that?" Ben asked.

"Doc McVickar traded in his car. The one he turned in is just like new. He bought it in December last year. The tires are real good and one of'em is new. Brand new!"

"Where is this good deal?" Ben asked.

"The place across the street from the bank. Just south of the bank." Bert knew where it was.

"Is that the Bank of Toronto or the Royal?" Ben knew that south of the Toronto was Heron's International Machinery lot. He was asking these questions while he was sorting out in his mind what Bert's big question would be, and what response would be needed.

"It is at George Hoffman's garage. The car is a 1926 Chevrolet Coupe, it is a pearl grey color with black fenders and I paid fifty dollars down. He will hold it till next Saturday night. Then I have to pay him the rest of the money." Bert had his head in the clouds over the Chev Coupe.

"How much money is that going to take?"

"The whole price was five hundred and fifty dollars, but I have already paid the fifty."

"How come George is selling that cheap?" Ben was not sold on the deal, and he could see the next question coming.

"George said that he had to charge the Doctor a big difference in the price, so he could sell the coupe to me so cheap." Bert had seen a good deal when it came his way.

Ben just waited.

Finally it came, "I make thirty dollars a month working here," Bert stated.

"Yes." Ben knew that.

"If you will give me five hundred dollars on Saturday and then keep twenty-five dollars a month out of my pay for twenty months, we would be squared up." Bert had figured this all out sometime during the night.

"But that will leave you five dollars a month to get by on."

"Oh, I can live on five dollars a month," Bert promised.

"A half pound tin of tobacco will cost you sixty-five cents."

"I know, but that still leaves me with four dollars and thirty-five cents." Bert was right up on his figures.

"Work boots will cost you three-fifty. Work pants will be close to three bucks." Ben knew figures too.

"I would not buy them both in the same month, so I will have no problem." Bert wanted that car.

"Well, we will see about it on Saturday," Ben promised.

The week that followed was most likely a happy one for Bert. Every thought revolved around the grey Chev coupe. On Saturday evening he got the five hundred dollar advance from his pay. Sunday morning the grey Chev coupe was parked by the bunkhouse. Bert had a disturbing thought. The gas tank was nearly dry. He was flat broke and it was ten days until the next pay day, and he would get only five dollars. On Wednesday evening Bert drove his new car to the crossroad one half a mile east and returned.

In September he moved it to a spot behind the bunkhouse. There he put it up on blocks and drained the radiator. The battery was removed and stored in the farm house cellar. It was in storage until spring. There was the odd autumn evening that Bert would sit in his car and have a final smoke of the day.

Most every night when the coal heater was banked for the night, Bert would be under the blankets on his cot. In the dark he would take fantasy trips in his new car. His suitcases would be in the trunk. On a beautiful day he would drive west past

Swift Current, past Maple Creek, through Medicine Hat, through Calgary and into the mountains. That would be as far as he would get that night, because then he would fall asleep.

Another night he would go to the Peace River country. He had worked with a guy that had been at Pouce Coupe. That would be a great trip to see unclaimed land!

The dreamland travels had become a hobby. Only so many more months and the car would be his, free and clear.

February had been a very bad month. Suddenly his needs were compounded. New leather pullover mitts with woolen liners, four buckle overshoes and a suit of woolen underwear. That cost more than five dollars. He was over drawn. No can of tobacco in February. He would have to go easy and string out January's can of fine cut. A person could roll from two hundred to two hundred and fifty cigarettes from a can of fine cut tobacco. With rough figures that would mean six or seven smokes a day for the month. After February the twenty-seventh Bert was rolling only one smoke in the evening. He would twist the paper on one end of his homemade cigarette so the tobacco dust would not fall out of the other end. He would push a small bit of cotton batten in the other end with a match stick. He then had a hot tasting filter tip cigarette.

March came as did the Canadian geese and a new tin of tobacco. The cold weather faded away and life was better for Bert.

A Sunday in July Bert put the battery in his car, let it down off the four firewood blocks and put water in the radiator. The battery was too weak to run the self starter so he had to crank the engine to get it started. He made the usual trip of one half mile east and back again.

Bert made that same trip in late September, and then put his car in winter storage. In November there were only four more months to pay on his car. The fantasy trips that he took every night before he went to sleep were getting richer and closer to the actual open road.

February the twenty-ninth, nineteen twenty-eight the Chevrolet coupe was his.

The last day of April Bert went to Ben, "Boss, I have sixty bucks. I quit. I want to go somewhere else."

Uncle Ben told me about Bert. "When he drove out of the yard that was the last I seen or heard of Bert Galant."

A few years later Berniece and I were married and living in Regina. We were looking for a house that newly weds could afford. A real estate dealer we met was Bert Galant.

"Mr. Galant, did you ever own a 1926 Chev coupe?"

He answered, "No."

That meant that this was not Uncle Ben's Bert.

The Sock Smuggler

Oh sure, I have had In Depth discussions with our police force while we were both parked on the shoulder of the highway.

The talk always went like this.

"You were driving 70 in a 50 zone."

"Yes, Sir."

"Do you think that it is wise to drive like that?"

"No, Sir."

He would talk.

"Yes, Sir."

He would talk again.

"No, Sir."

After this brilliant exchange of ideas, we each went on our way.

I have had conversations with the law where I would just listen.

I was leaning against the body shop foreman's desk. One morning an officer of an out of town detachment came to the shop desk.

"Last night, some low life person took a beer bottle cap and scratched the fender on one of our cars. Could you repair it today?"

I looked it over and my thought was that it could be ready by mid afternoon.

"Great. Can I get a ride to the court house?"

I used my car and drove him and his briefcase to the halls of justice.

It was after the noon hour, that the Mountie came back for his car. The scratch had been sanded out, primed, polished and painted. It was a matter of having the infra red light on the fender, to quick dry the paint. Those were the good old days, but it took a long time to dry paint.

"It looks good to me. When will it be ready?" said the officer as he inspected the fresh paint.

"In forty-five minutes it will be finished." I moved the portable rack of light bulbs back a few inches to properly finish baking the fresh paint.

We stood waiting and were watching the paint bake on the RCMP car. Our conversation turned to the strange little things that crop up in a lifetime.

The police officer told of his stopping a smuggler.

"At one time I was stationed at a town on the international boarder. On the United States side there was a horseshoe shaped road that went a mile west of the highway and led back to the custom office. On the Canadian side there was a hill, with rose bushes, and assorted brush growing on the top of it.

One afternoon I lay up there with my note book and field glasses. It was not long until a black Oldsmobile took the road from the pavement. He stopped right below me. He was so close that I could have tossed a pebble down on his car.

This guy was alone. He got out and opened the trunk and brought out a J.C.Penney's shopping bag. He sat on the edge of the car seat with the door open, he removed his shoes. He opened the bag and took out a pair of red socks. At the time Penney's stores were selling those thin cotton socks for seven cents a pair."

I had to interrupt. "Before we were married, my wife bought her brother and I each a pair of Penney socks. We wore them to a dance one night. When the night was over, so was the life of the socks. The feet were wore out."

The Mountie laughed, "Yes, that would be the same kind that my smuggler had in his bag. What color did you guys have?"

Anyway the fellow put on the red socks, then a pair of blue ones, then yellow, then green, then white, and at last black. This international traveler was wearing seven pair of socks. He threw away the empty bag and drove away.

I went on a usual patrol. It was about thirty miles from the boarder that I saw the same black Oldsmobile gaining on me. I turned on my light and stopped him.

"Your driver's licence, please?"

He fumbled and got his license out.

"Where are you going?"

"Home."

"Where have you been?"

"In the States."

"Did you declare anything at the port of entry?"

"No, nothing."

"How about the six extra pair of socks you have on?" I asked him.

At first he was nervous. Now he just sat there rather numb.

"What socks?" he asked.

"The black and white and green and yellow and blue and red socks that you have on."

"What do you mean?"

I told him to just pull up his pant leg, and, I turned the sock tops down one at a time and named the colors for him. He was somewhat shook up.

"I did not tell the custom's officer about my socks."

"Well, you know that you were smuggling socks into Canada, because you did not declare them when you entered the country. I will let you off with a warning this time if you will take this ticket back to the customs and have them sign it after you have shown them your new socks."

He got his car turned back to the south, but then stopped.

"How did you know about my socks?" he asked.

"I am an officer of the Royal Canadian Mounted Police. We know everything."

"He drove away both relieved and still confused, to go back and declare forty-two cents worth of cotton socks."

Courage

To do what has to be done sometimes takes a large amount of courage.

It happened on a snapping cold night.

Dale and Doris Daniels and their two girls live at Chitek Lake. Dale's boyhood home is about thirty miles away.

It was a few miles from that home where Dale had a hunter's tree stand beside a game trail. Hunting season was past. It was time to get the stand down out of the tree. Dale loaded the snow machine into his new Dodge truck.

"I am going to get my tree stand home."

"Can I come along"? Eight year old Jolene asked.

"Well, you will have to put warm clothes on. It is very cold outside," her father answered.

It was near eight o'clock when Dale drove down the bush trail and turned the truck around. It took some see sawing back and forth on the narrow trail to get the truck facing the way out. This was done so the ski doo could be unloaded for the half mile trip into the forest to where the tree stand was.

One good pull on the starter rope and the little engine came to life. Dale sat on the snow machine and Jolene sat behind her Dad. It was a matter of minutes and they were at the tree stand.

Dale climbed the tree and began to undo the platform. Jolene just stood and admired the beauty of the forest on a winter night.

There was a crash as Dale fell 20 feet to the ground. A frozen Aspen limb had snapped off and Dale lay on the ground with his body paralyzed.

"Dad, get up."

"I can't move and I can't feel anything ."

"Dad, it is so cold we have to go home."

"Jolene, take the ski doo and go to Grandpa's and get help."

The little girl rushed over to the snowmobile, turned on the ignition key and gave the starter rope a pull. Nothing happened. She was not strong enough to make the engine turn over to start.

"I can't get it started, Dad."

"Go to the truck and drive slow to Grandpa's."

"I have never driven the truck, Dad," her voice had a hint of desperation.

"That is all right, Jolene. Tonight you will drive O. K." Dale reassured her.

With a series of runs, walks and runs again she reached the truck. She knew how serious the plight was for her Dad.

Jolene got in the truck cab. She had to stand and rest against the truck seat. The engine started as it was supposed to do. She pulled the shift leaver into drive, then stood on one foot while she stepped on the gas pedal with the other, and look through the spokes on the steering wheel. She was driving, and on the way to Grandpa's. There were places that she had to speed up a bit just like Dad would do, so the truck would not slip backwards on the snow and ice.

Out of the forest and on the gravel road. So far so good. At the turn in Grandpa's driveway, the truck slid to the right.The front wheel dropped off the edge of the road, and Jolene was stuck. She turned off the switch key and left the truck. She ran flat out the remaining distance to the house.

Out of breath, she opened the door and gasped, "Come and help Dad. He is going to freeze to death if we don't get there quick."

In his truck with Uncle Lou driving, and this time, Jolene sitting on the seat between Uncle and Grandpa, directed the rescue party.

In a couple of days the Canadian Broadcasting Corporation had spread the story of Jolene and her heroism across the nation. Dale spent weeks in The Royal University Hospital in Saskatoon and then was well on his way to recovery.

The story of Jolene's heroism must have been carried on the French network. She, Jolene, received a letter from an eighty year old lady that lives in Montreal. She congratulated Jolene on her bravery and the inspiration that she brought to others.

"After seeing you on television, I thought that if an eight year old girl had that much courage, why shouldn't I study and take my driver's test. Now I have my driver's licence. Thanks to you."

Birding

There was Joe's Grocery on the corner. The red brick Oddfellows Hall was beside Joe's. Then the big cotton wood tree, Grahams telephone office, the post office and the bank were all situated on the west side of the street.

Renfield Graham was a sharp minded citizen that lived next to the big cotton wood tree. He was ten years old and the fellow that you would vote the most likely to succeed. At dusk he saw the sparrows hopping into an eavestrough spout for a night's rest.

The birds did it the next night, too.

Opportunity knocked so Ren answered. He found two clear plastic bags and was ready for daylight. In the wee early hours he climbed up, slipped a bag over the end of the rain spout. Tapping gently on the pipe with a stick he soon had the birds awake. Moments later he had a bag of sparrows. He went down the ladder and into the house with his bag of birds. Ren had fourteen birds. He set up six cups on the kitchen table. You may ask six cups for fourteen birds?

Well, he had only six food color bottles to work with, so six cups.

It took very little time to mix the cupfuls of dye. Mother Graham may not give her stamp of approval to the project.

The first sparrow got held by the feet. He was dunked head first into the cup of red dye. With its wings it mixed the liquid in the cup. The bird man figured that was a good thing. The red bird was shoved into the second plastic bag to dry off.

The blue, yellow, green, pink and purple birds followed into the bag to let their color set up and dry off. There were two of each color so the last two birds got blended experimental colors. They looked great. In fact all of the birds had an exotic look.

The mail would be sorted and in the post office boxes by nine o'clock. School would start at nine. The coffee crowd would leave the café so they could get their mail at nine. Many ladies would also pass the big cottonwood tree going for their mail just before nine o'clock.

Seven minutes to nine was the hour to strike. Then Ren took the bag of colored birds to the back door and let them go. The sparrows, after their dip into a cup of food coloring were ever so relieved to see daylight and the familiar cottonwood tree.

Helen and Dorothy were the first ladies to pass the Oddfellows Hall.

"Look at the red bird in the tree!"

"And there is a blue bird and a canary."

These sightings soon had a group of bird watchers collected on the sidewalk. Joe and Charlie came from the café just as the pretty birds flew across the street to another tree.

Joe who had farmed and studied nature on the land noted, "They have a lot of color but fly like sparrows."

Our Bird Man left the window where he had watched the bird watchers. With a smirk he snuck across the back lane and was only a few minutes late for school.

Smart Girl

Bill and I sat on the running board of a 1949 one ton Chev truck. It was on a warm sunny afternoon in September. We were soaking in the sunshine on the back lot of Enerson Motors in Lethbridge, Alberta. We sat there because work was slack. The city folks were driving carefully, and the farm and ranch people were too busy at that time of year to worry about dents in their cars or trucks.

"It was a day like this ten years ago, when Jack and I sat waiting for the company's Dodge Power Wagon to come and pick us up. There was a crew of us a way up in the Yukon Territory checking out a site for a mine camp. Well, the job was complete, and we were supposed to get out for the winter. We had a company bus down at the highway, and that was a long ways away. There was only so much room in the Dodge, and Jack and I were the least important of the team, so we got left when the first trip went out. Our orders were to take down the tents, and have every thing packed to load when the truck came back the next day. We did not mind too much at being in the same class as the tents and other gear, but it was kind of a draggy morning. It was about nine-thirty when we were all packed up.

Jack said, "Let's walk down the trail and meet the Dodge. It will be something to do."

We had walked for most of an hour when we heard a buzz. Here came a U.S. Army jeep along the edge of a moose meadow. The green Jeep had been painted orange with a big brush, and in a hurry, too, the way it looked. The fella stopped and asked us where we were going? We said Alberta.

"Well, climb in. My plane is down here about five miles, and I'm flying to Calgary."

Jack thought that would be good. He could take a bus home to Edmonton. I would take the bus to Lethbridge, and be home that night.

Well, that is just the way it worked. We hitch hiked by plane to Calgary, and then took the bus. I got home at eleven o'clock that night. At eight the next morning, I phoned the office in Calgary to let them know where I was.

The manager there said, 'Get in your car and go to Grassy right away.' He meant, the mine at Grassy Lake, Alberta.

The day before they had something break at the mine and had to shut down. I was supposed to go and fix it, and work there for the winter.

I found a house, so my wife and I lived in Grassy for a few months. I had worked there for at least six weeks when two of the Hot Shots came from Calgary. We called them Hot Shots because their department knew everything. Boy! Oh Boy! Did they ever climb all over my frame.

"So here you are, and we have spent thousands of dollars searching all over the Yukon for you two guys. We should take that cost out of your pay."

I shrugged my shoulders and said, "We have a very smart girl in the office. Why didn't you ask her? She has sent me my paychecks here ever since I was sent here to the mine."

Bad Boys

Her name was Mrs. Tillie Mylnko, but to the whole town and countryside she was Baba. As a teen age girl she came to Canada from a district on the edge of the Ukraine. There was not a plant that that woman could not make grow better. She was very good at bumps and bruises that little people can gather so often. With a quiet smile that lady could win any number of friends.

Mrs. M. had great command of English, Oh there was the odd time with the odd word that you would detect a trace of an accent, but as you spent a few minutes with Tilly, the accent disappeared.

Any time you hear of an accent in some one's speech, you might bet that they know something that you don't.

The memory of where we were that evening escapes me, but I remember that we had finished a great dinner and were stuffed like poisoned puppies.

The chain of conversation must have led Baba to remember her brother's escapades.

.

"In old country we had a neighbor with a big huge apple tree. Oh so many apples, they would fall on the ground and be lost. When the apples were big and red and juicy the boys would go and steal them off of the tree. This old man was cross, and he would wave his walking stick and shout at the boys. His apples always went to waste but he did not want anyone else to eat them. One night he took his jug of plum brandy and a blanket and sat by his tree to guard his many apples. The boys watched him and when he fell asleep they got the old man on his blanket. They took the edge of the blanket and four guys holding the blanket on each side they carried him to the grave yard and laid him among the tomb stones. When he woked up------------- -------------- --------------- -- ------------ ---------- -------------- ----------."

Baba got so involved with her story that the next paragraph was told in her eastern European language

Mrs. Mylnko at eighty years of age had a figure that many young women would envy. Slim trim and energetic. The laughter that she followed the story with, shook her body. It was so funny an ending.

Wiping away a laughter tear she reverted to English, "They was bad boys."

I could not understand the Ukrainian language. I felt that it would break the spell to have her repeat it all in English.

I never did find out how bad the boys were.

A Holiday

It was the year of Saskatchewan's seventy-fifth birthday. That would make it in 1980.

Our daughter Margaret or Maggie as she is known to the rest of the world, and two of her friends took time away from home for a little holiday. They saddled up their horses and with packs behind the saddles, started riding south west.

Maggie was riding her horse Mohawk, Meryl had Mare and Sandy rode her horse Bambie.

Mohawk was a tall skittish pinto horse that had a family background more varied than the children of an ancient conquered nation. One grandmother was a pinto Shetland pony. One grandfather was a Tennessee Walker. His father was an English Thoroughbred. He inherited a trait from each ancestor. The color and longevity, were from his Shetland grandmother. The ability to go and go and go was from the Tennessee horse. The jumpy rattle headed stupidity, I suppose he got from the Thoroughbred.

Don and Irene Taylor gave the pinto colt to cousin Marilyn Muri. Mohawk was about eleven years old when the Muri family left the farm, and Marilyn was off to make her way in the world.

Marilyn riding her horse Mohawk, came for a ride with Margaret who rode a grey Shetland pony. They switched mounts along the trail and when they returned, Marilyn looked underprivileged riding the grey Shetland pony, but Margaret looked just the opposite on the tall pinto.

Marilyn asked her smaller eleven year old cousin, "Do you like Mohawk?"

With a super smile and a breathless answer, Margaret said, "Oh, yes."

Marilyn handed the reins to Margaret and said , "He is yours." It was a still day. A slight breeze would have knocked the smaller cousin over. She was dumbfounded with such a gift.

Margaret and Mohawk were pals for twenty-one more years. He was partly responsible for her love of riding.

Maggie and her two friends started out on their ride to go to the Cypress Hills Park. Their home base was around Shellbrook, Saskatchewan. That was four hundred miles from the Park.

The first few days were very hot, windy and dusty. The fourth day a big obstacle was the railroad overpass southwest of Saskatoon. They picked the hour of daybreak to ride across it. When the girls got there it looked like a never ending line of diesel powered semi-trailers using number seven highway. They took the lower approach. They just rode across the railroad track. No fence and no bother.

Both horses and riders were getting tired. Meryl had a friend living at Pike Lake. That was good for a three day rest.

Back on the trail, the tired feeling was still with them. Fifty miles down the road Mare was dragging her feet. Her horse's reaction to the holiday was not a comfort to Meryl.

Sandy who was also losing her enthusiasm or becoming adverse to saddle sores, came up with a new plan.

"If we could find a place to leave Mare, Meryl could ride Bambie and I will catch a Greyhound for Edmonton."

At Harris the new plan was carried out. Sandy took the bus and a local horse woman kept Mare for them.

This was not a well-equipped safari. The girls carried their supplies with them. Tent, food and toothbrush. They had no pack horse or truck to carry horse feed. They came to an area of parched grass and nothing for a horse to eat, There was one lonesome grain elevator beside the railroad track. They rode to it. The elevator manager stepped out of his office.

Maggie asked, "Could you sell us a bushel of oats?"

"No."The answer was gruff and definite.

"Is there a farm yard with some grass that our horses could have?"

Another No.

The gentleman thought that he should learn a little bit about these girls that appeared to be poor Gypsies. He asked, "Where are you from?"

Maggie answered, "Shellbrook."

"I had dealings with a man from Shellbrook at one time, and he was a good honest person," the elevator man mentioned.

"Who was that?" Maggie asked.

"His name is Ed Mumm, and he is a good guy."

"He was my husband's father," Maggie said in a soft voice.

"Whatcha mean was?" the man grumbled.

"He died in an accident on icy roads two years before I married his son Jim."

What a change came over the man. It was a shock to him to learn of Ed Mumm's passing.

"So if he was living, you would be Ed's daughter-in-law?" he asked.

Maggie just nodded her answer with a lump in her throat.

"Could you tell us where there is a leaf cutter bee farmer near here?" Maggie asked.

The elevator man pointed to a grove of trees a mile away.

The next morning these kind people gave the rest of a bag of oats to the girls. Then phoned friends that lived about twenty miles southwest, and arranged for a night's stopping place for the girls.

That happened again and again. Maggie and company were handed from one farm to the next. They were beyond Rosetown, Saskatchewan when their horses took a wrong idea and the lucky chain was broken. They had stopped to rest. Their mounts were standing with their heads just hanging down. A horse fly or a bad thought sent the horses running down the road. The only good thing about it was that they were running in the direction of Cypress Hills Park.

Along the north side of the South Saskatchewan River the trail ran up and down through the breaks (sharp sided coulees). Mohawk lost his skittishness. He looked the worse for wear when the girls rode into a ranch yard late that afternoon. They were made welcome.

"May we pitch our tent in the yard and stay for the night?" Maggie asked.

"You can stay for the night but no tent," the ranch owner stated. "With that gang of clowns that stay in the bunkhouse, the tent would not be a good place to sleep. Their practical jokes would only be part of the cowboy shenanigan. We have plenty of room in the house for you ladies."

After supper the talk turned to horses. The host mentioned that he had bought a Quarter Horse from Arling Newton.

In a surprised voice Maggie said, "Oh, he is my Dad's cousin." Then family got mixed in with the horse talk.

At the breakfast table the rancher said, "Your pinto is in need of a rest. I have a horse that needs some riding. I would like to see you take him for the rest of your trip."

Maggie said, "But, it is a long way to Cypress from here, I would not feel right about using your horse for that long a ride."

He replied, "It is a hundred miles from here to the hills. It would do my horse good if you rode him that far in one day."

The five or six ranch hands that ate at the table had some smirky looks as they shoved in the bacon, eggs and hot cakes.

At the corral Mohawk still looked very tired. The big bay horse was tied in the corral as the Boss had directed one of the cowboys.

This horse that was supposed to be good for a hundred miles a day did seem to be anxious to be somewhere else. He did not take too kindly to being saddled. While Maggie was cinching up, he kept dancing around as far as the short halter shank would allow. She was continuously dancing, too, to keep from having her toes stepped on. Added to the action of the horse there were faces of the cowboys peeking around corners and between the corral rails. Under her breath Maggie said, "Well horse! It's you or I. One of us will win." She pulled his head to the left with the bridle and swung on.

"Please open the gate," Maggie asked.

The bay horse with his head held high by tight firm reins trotted smartly down the road.

As she and Meryl left the ranch to ride the last hundred miles, there were hats waved in a mixture of farewell and congratulations.

Farther down the road they stopped at a ranch before they crossed the river. The house was run by the ranch wife. Her mother was second in command. During the evening the Grandmother watched Maggie during every conversation. At last she spoke.

"Young lady, you just remind me so much of one of my college chums that it is remarkable."

"What was your friend's name?" Maggie asked.

"Oh, that was Olga Muri that I went to college with."

"Well, for goodness sake. She is my grandmother," Maggie said.

From then on the talk was between the Grandmother and Maggie.

Miles and miles more of riding. The day was done, the girls could not make it all of the way to the Cypress Park before dark, so they stopped at a ranch and asked for permission to camp in their yard.

The tall slim white haired man with the work bent bones and suntanned face had other ideas.

"No, ladies, you will be our guests. There is no need of tenting here. Mother and I have plenty of room in the house for you."

Meryl and Maggie were escorted into the house and introduced to the rancher's wife. They had entered another world. Every room was fashioned as of a hundred years ago. The couple had been married for seventy years. They furnished their home as newly weds with the things of that period, and it was still beautiful.

Bedtime came. The lady of the house showed the girls to their room. The only change in seventy years was the electric light. When the hostess switched on the light, low and behold, a sparkling white bedroom of the last century. Lace and frills and starch. Everything in the room was old and exquisite.

"With our dirty clothes and boots we can not stay in this room."

"Oh yes, you are so welcome to spend the night here. It has been a long time since we have had company that could stay over night. Just go in and make yourselves at home." The lady was sincere.

"No, it will be too much work for you folks to clean up after us. We will put up our tent," both Maggie and Meryl insisted.

The next night they slept in their tent in Cypress Park.

Do's and Don't's
for the next four hundred mile ride

- Use younger horses.
- Condition horses with more than a two mile run every night.
- Close saddle bags before letting the horses run away from you.
- Do not cue a cutting horse by just stretching your legs.
- Ride in a tight little circle when starting out a horse that may buck.
- Don't lose the last ten dollar bill in a friendly ranch wife's washing machine.
- Don't tie a horse to a tree that has old barbwire in the rose brush beside it.
- Try to sleep on dry saddle pads.
- Double check when husbands will be there with the stock trailer to pick you up.

Team Work

There had been a shortage of rain for a few years when we were kids about seventy years ago. The soil on prairie farm yards was hard, bare, dark grey and cracked. Foot and wheel traffic soon destroyed grass and weeds, and that was why the ground was in that condition.

Aunt Emma Newton decided that her ground around the house did not have to look so desolate. She had it plowed and cultivated, and turned it into a beautiful flower bed.

Eleanor and Woodrow were the younger Newton children. She was eleven years old and he was seven.

Princess was a great big black Percheron mare. If she would have been human, she would have been a Saint. Her manners were wonderful, and her understanding of people's wishes were what made her great.

The garden cultivator was a new relative of the walking plow. Like the plow it had two handles for the worker to guide the thing with. The working part was six or seven pointed shovels a few inches wide. A small metal wheel at the front (and some machines had one on the back, too) were to control the depth of the cultivator. A single horse was hooked to the front of the cultivator to pull it through the garden. The cultivator could be adjusted from two to three feet wide to suite the space between the rows in the garden.

Flower bed, kids, horse and cultivator were all brought together one afternoon at the Newton farm.

Princess was harnessed and hitched to the cultivator. Woodrow's job was to ride and guide the horse. Eleanor was at the handles of the cultivator. Her job was to guide the machine to kill the weeds and save the flowers.

The sun was bright and hot, and the flower bed was getting a good working over. The soil was turning up with a rich brown color, and the green weeds with their roots exposed to the air were wilting.

The flowers were not in regimented straight rows. Aunt had curves and turns in the paths that her son and daughter were cleaning the weeds from. There were little islands of colorful flowers.

To maneuver through this garden of flowers took skill on the part of the horseman as well as skill by the cultivator operator. It was getting hot and boring. Woodrow's attention span was wearing thin.

"Woodrow be careful! You had Princess step on a Petunia. Woodrow stop that. Now we dug out a Marigold," Eleanor directed from behind the cultivator.

Woodrow's reaction was to make Princess trot. With the faster pace Eleanor was not able to control her end of things. Weeds were getting missed, and flowers were getting rooted up.

"Woodrow, stop right now!"

Woodrow slid off the horse and made a dash for the house. He called over his shoulder, "You can do this by yourself."

Eleanor had different ideas. She tackled her brother. Woodrow was on his back in the dirt. He said a bad word. His sister had two reasons to straighten out her little brother. Swearing was one and the second was that she had to have help to clean up the patch of flowers. There was no weapon of any description within reach, so she grabbed a big lump of dirt. This was used as a mouth wash on her work mate.

Princess stood calmly by while the difference of opinion was thrashed out. Woodrow climbed back on the horse and the work continued.

In later years she remembered, "Dad always seemed to favor his youngest son, but after Mom and Dad had gone to bed, I heard her tell Dad about the fight Woodrow and I had had in the afternoon. I heard Dad laugh, and then I knew that I was home free"

Aunt Emma's flower garden in front of the house was as big as a lot for a city home.

I remember it sure looked beautiful.

No Accident Just a Mishap

We lived in Lethbridge, Alberta then. I worked at Enerson Motors body shop. The auto body shop was with the truck branch on Ninth Ave. N, just at the foot of the overpass.

The tow truck had just brought the 1955 Ford car from the frame repair shop. It was brought back to my work stall. It had the Mounted Police logo on each front door. There was fresh black paint on the frame right up to the body mounts. There was the engine sitting right where it was supposed to be, above the new cross member and all of those other new parts.

My job was to put on the rest of the new parts like hood, fenders, radiator, grill, bumper and windshield on the black car. Our parts pickup truck had just brought me all of those pieces. They made quite a pile in my corner. I was figuring out a plan of attack when a Royal Canadian Mounted Police officer walked in. It was Berniece's cousin Bob.

After a minute's greeting Bob said, "I can tell you all about this wreck."

"It was three weeks ago that one of the Mounties and I had a week end off. We decided to go to Great Falls for a couple of days. At nine o'clock that night, we stopped at the Cardston detachment to say Hello to the guys. There were two patrols going out. It was a quiet Friday night so my buddy and I split up and went with each car.

The Steve guy that I was with had driven to the edge of town when a car careened around a corner. It skidded back and forth in a fishtail fashion, then straightened out and went down a gravel road real fast. We followed. We were both going about seventy miles an hour. Our top light was on and so was the siren. The car in front went even faster. They were a few hundred yards ahead of us when they disappeared. There was a curve in the road, but the car we were after had shot straight on down a dirt road. That was why we thought that it had disappeared for a bit.

Steve could not make the curve in the road at the speed we were going, so he was pumping the brakes to slow down. He did not make it to a stop. We slid over the edge of the road and into the ditch among some big rocks. Those rocks brought us to a sudden stop. Steve and I got out to have a look at the car. The front end was smashed and the front wheels were under the driver's seat.

We looked over to the left and there was the Buick , sitting in a slough with its wheels covered with water. Its driver we wanted to warn about the reckless driving. There were seven teenage boys in the car.

Steve radioed to the detachment for the wagon, two pair of hand cuffs and someone with hipwaders. It was but a few minutes until the paddy wagon came. The boys were soon hand cuffed one to the next. They were a wet downcast chain of prisoners that were led out of the water. They spent the night in jail and in the morning were taken home to face the music.

Trail Blazers

I was well into the parkland. It was too early for hunting, because the moose season would not be open for three weeks. I was just nosing around to see if this would be a good area to come back to when the season did open.

At the local watering hole I asked a couple of guys at the next table.

"Well, now if yu'r from the city the best thing you could do is to go and talk to Joe or Jake. They could help you find game. They are undisputed experts on local game birds and animals, weather, outer space and other things."

"Where do I find these pillars of wisdom?" I asked.

"Well, let me see. You go east of town til you cross the bridge, then turn north. You follow that trail for about twenty miles. At the end of it you should find one or the other."

The bar keep had a stupid grin that he was trying to cover up when I paid for a thank you round for the helpful gentlemen.

Turning off the highway there were ruts, rocks, stumps and even windfall across the road. It was a struggle to keep going but then it was early afternoon and I would not want to miss a good thing. That was the longest roughest twenty miles that I had seen in a long time. It led away into the back woods.

Joe Smonds sat on an upended block of Birch fire wood. I had a similar seat. Joe talked. I listened.

"It seemed that they were blazing a trail from their old planet away over to the right of us. They were traveling right by us on earth and going on into the fourth galaxy over to the west.

Now the guy in the first ship knew that he would have to make a sharp turn a few billion miles from here so he swooped down and grabbed one of my neighbour Jake's pigs. Well, they put the pig on some kind of a little platform there in outer space. The message to the next ship would be. TURN AT THE PIG.

You know how temperamental pigs are. When the next ship came along, the darn pig took off like a scared rabbit. It just got lost. Well, seeing as they still had a lot of trail blazing to do, they swiped another pig from Jake. He just lives around that bush over there and across the ridge. That pig was just like the first one. When they opened the door, the pig just went nuts and ran away.

Jake only had two pigs so the next time them guys come they took Jake himself. Well, when they set Jake on the little platform that was invisible, he did not run. He stayed put. Soon after that time they had the trail on computer cards. They could slip a card in the instrument panel and, swish, they could travel like on automatic pilot.

When the route was all settled, they were going to let Jake stay where he was. They figured that Jake would run away like the rest of the markers. You know the pigs were just scared. That was why they ran away. Jake was scared, too, but different. They stopped to pick him up and he grabbed onto the first space man close to him. Dern near choked the poor guy. They had to shoot him with a dark gun to settle poor old Jake down so they could load him up.

When they shot him with the dark gun, Jake said that everything went black.

"I can just about see Jake's chimney from here. There hadn't been any smoke for four days so I went over to see if he was all right.

Jake had been taken along to the new planet. He was put in a little room by himself. It was like a big umbrella. Sometimes he could see the walls and other times the walls were invisible, but he could not walk through the walls even if he could not see them. There was only one fella that came to see him or feed him. Every so often the guy brought him a tall glass of something that was like a milk shake made of water and sand. The drink seemed healthy enough, but it had no taste.

These people were smaller than a big man and bigger than a small man. They had no clothes and no distinguishing parts of their bodies. They were a grey color with tan arms and legs. After a while Jake saw different ones. They were the same but had green arms and some of them carried little ones like themselves. Jake figured that they were wimmen, but their bodie's were the same as the others only with green arms.

Well, Jake soon got tired of drinking them sand shakes, so he belly ached for coffee. He wanted toast and coffee, then he wanted ham and eggs, then mashed potatoes and gravy. His keeper got tired of Jake's complaining. He went to the big boss.

'Toast, coffee, ham, eggs, mashed gravy, potatoes.' The tan armed fellow was at a loss.

'What is all this stuff that the trail marker animal wants?'

The big boss had enough on his mind with getting the new planet all livable so he said,

'Load the critter in the Zip Ship and take it back were we found it. Remember to put the card in with the silver circle up. That will take you right to the spot. When you dump off the animal, turn the card over and the little ship will bring you home again .'

"Well, the day I went to check on Jake, there was a swish sound and this cigar and swallow tailed plane stopped at Jake's pig pin. Jake tumbled out. The guy in the driver's seat fumbled with something on the dash board. Another swish and it was gone."

"Jake don't keep pigs no more. He fixed up the fence and plants garden there and he keeps goats now."

Old Joe with his droopy handle bar mustache surmised, "All living things are natchurly scared. The pigs were scared of anything that moved. Jake was scared of falling off into space."

Joe ended with, "It is sure too bad that nobody believes any thing Jake says any more."

Step on the Gas, Rabbit

In the year 1930 there was not much money on the prairies but there were lots of big long eared Jack Rabbits. Many boys that were old enough to use a .22 rifle, and in those days they did not have to be very old, hunted rabbits. Rabbits were caught and their pelts were shipped to Sidney I. Robinson, fur buyer in Winnipeg, Manitoba. The first claim on the fur cheque was likely new bicycle tires. If there was money left over, there were things leftover, too.

Berniece and I were sitting around the kitchen table with Joann and Norman at the Wood's house. The subject of rabbits came up. The cotton tails had eaten the bark off Berniece's rose bush.

Norman said, "I had a wild experience with a Jack Rabbit."

"I was just a wee fella, maybe seven years old. Dad had helped me make a dog harness out of discarded horse harness. We had a big black collie dog with a white ring around his neck. My sleigh had a wooden apple box fastened on it. I would get the dog hitched to my sleigh and climb into the box, and when I was sitting in the box, my knees were up near my chin. The dog would trot around the yard and I would have a good little sleigh ride.

It was on a nice bright morning in February that I hitched up the dog. We were just touring around the farmyard when a big old Jack Rabbit came hopping along.

I hollered, "Step on the gas, Rabbit." He did and so did the dog. What a ride! If the rabbit ducked to the side where the snow was light, my sleigh would skid sideways around the corner. The rabbit had his long ears right down tight against his neck. He was running fast. The dog was running as fast as he could with me and the sleigh skimming or bouncing along behind him. The longer the chase the more exciting my ride got. I nearly got wiped out when the rabbit went past the corner of the barn. A few more turns and the sleigh tipped over on its side, and I fell out. With me out of the box, the sleigh tipped back up on the level and the dog picked up speed. In no time they were out of sight. I figured that the dog would catch the rabbit and maybe bring him home in the box."

"He didn't."

The Last Kernel

We had gone to sundown feeding for the cow herd. At daylight I would walk through the bunch of cows, lying chewing their cuds. If everything was normal it left me with lot of idle hours. I filled in that time by going to town and fixing trucks for Bud Zimmer at his Venture Farm Truck Sales shop.

One day a couple came and made a deal on the red Chev one ton with the steel box and hoist. There were a few things to be done to it before the truck was ready for sale. The lady forgot a pair of knitted woolen gloves on the desk in the show room. I put them in one of the drawers. Her husband came for the truck and I handed him the gloves. Ed, the mechanic, still had an hour or so to finish the work on the truck. That gave Mr. Wilson, the new owner of the truck, and I, time for a visit.

We were both from the Swift Current area.

He told me, "In 1931 the crop was very poor south of Swift Current. Dad come north to find a better place to farm. He did get land in Ladder Valley and it had a cabin on it. Mother wanted to go as soon as Dad got back with the news. Us boys were ready to come at that time, too."

No! Dad felt that he would need the money from the crop to get us up north. Well, that crop consisted of mostly bare ground, some weeds and a few straws of wheat here and there. We were packing and planning, and watching the wheat to see if it would not be ripe enough to harvest. The Russian thistles grew and ripened. Their thorns were sure a nuisance when we did walk through the field to look for ripe yellow straws of wheat. Mother said that we should leave the crop and travel north while the weather was good. Dad said that he would not leave his last crop at Wymark. We lived about two miles south west of the town. There were two wagons already loaded. Mom was anxious to get started. "No we are going to need the money from the crop," Dad said and he would not change his mind.

The day finally came when Dad hitched four horses on the binder and began the harvest. It was a heartbreaking job for him. He would cut a patch here and another over there. Well, it was finally threshed and hauled to the elevator. I think that Dad got around sixty-five dollars for the whole crop. There was still the last bit of packing to do. There was the stuff out of the house that went in the last wagon. Dad did not seem to hurry. I suppose that he hated to leave the farm that had promised so much in earlier years.

Everything was packed in the wagons so the house was no longer livable. There were three teams on wagons, and the herd of cows to get on the road. We made real good time the first three days. That night we camped two miles south of Stewart Valley. We woke up in the morning to see a heavy snow fall. We stayed right where we were. It snowed all day. Before it quit there was a good two feet of snow on the ground. That was followed by a light rain, and then the weather turned bitterly cold. There was a two inch crust of ice on the snow.

We camped there while we waited for the rail cars to get to Stewart Valley. When we did get the cars, it was a terrible two miles for the livestock to walk. Their legs were bleeding for being cut by the ice.

When we got to Big River and were all set to go to the new farm, Dad used the last of his money to buy one box of .22 rifle shells. He shot nine deer that winter so we did live pretty good.

Rabbit got Home Free

It was a late fall evening. The sun was down and the breeze was cool. Earl had asked me to come to the farm and have a look at his truck troubles. I advised him how to have his local welder make up reinforcing plates and install them.

"Your troubles are not all that bad. When those trucks were a year or two old, I have done two in a day." And I wasn't even bragging.

A coyote out a mile from the yard gave out a lusty howl. Two of Earl's grandsons that were city boys, came racing around the corner of the building.

These boys were four and six years old, and at the moment had large round eyes.

"Grandpa, what is making that awful scary noise?"

Just then the coyote let rip another scary noise.

Earl sat on an upended pail and motioned for me to sit on a wooden crate that was about the right height.

"That is a coyote howling," he told the boys.

"Why do they howl?" asked the smaller guy.

"When I was small an Indian man told me about them."

"What did he say, Grandpa?" they both wanted to know.

Many years ago, before there were cars and cities and no body lived here, the coyote did not howl. He had a small singing voice. You boys remember the three fields where we made hay. On one side of the first field there was a huge log lying on the ground. Three rabbits had their home just behind the log. Charles, the first one, had gone across the field to eat some willow bark. Before he got finished with his lunch, the coyote came along. Charlie's brothers were peeking over the log and saw the coyote.

Richard said, "Our brother may be in trouble. The coyotes is sniffing around."

Wallace said, "You go to the next field and I will go to the third one. We will fool the coyote."

Charles was hopping home from the willow bush when the coyote saw him. The coyote licked his lips once and ran to catch the rabbit. Charles ran around the edge of the field and the coyote ran after him. Coyotes can run farther than rabbits can. The snow was deep and Charles was getting tired. When he saw Richard hiding nearby he raised one of his rabbit ears. That signaled his brother that he would run one more time around the field but then he would need help. Around they came and there was Richard running in the track. Charles sneaked off to the side and went home.

Richard ran around the second field with the coyote after him. When he got tired, he held up one ear. He made one more trip around the field and Wallace crossed the track and the coyote chased him. They went around the third field many times and the coyote was so tired that he stop running. He thought that he had been chasing one rabbit, and he had to give up. When he got up on the hill near his home, he cried because he was so hungry and did not have a rabbit for his dinner.

"That is why coyotes howl or cry now," Earl finished.

The older brother was mentally digesting this tale. The four year old with a look of Solomon's wisdom asked,

"Is the coyote still hungry Grandpa?"

The Rescue Crew

It was in the winter of 1943. The snow was deep. None of us school students from out of town had been home since New Year's. One afternoon there was a green half ton truck parked in front of the café. That was the first sign of spring we had seen.

Boyd Anderson from Glentworth, Saskatchewan had come to see his sisters, Verna, who was teaching the lower grades and Lyla, a grade twelve student. Boyd was on his way to serve in the Royal Canadian Air Force.

That was a gloomy time across Canada. The war correspondents not only had to dodge bombs and bullets but they had a hard time to find a news item that would cheer the folks back home. Germany, Italy and Japan seemed to have the upper hand. That was why Boyd was going to help.

Mr. Cliff Peart, the school principal, did not feel any better about the war, but he did not let it smother his humor. He kept his math and science classes as interesting as only he could do.

He told of Prowler to back up the law of falling bodies. If a ball were dropped from the roof of a sky scraper, every foot would increase its speed according to the formula in the book.

I do not remember the formula, but I do remember Prowler's story.

A family that lived in a small town northeast of Regina thought that they owned Prowler. Little did they know that Prowler owned them and the rest of the town.

It was on a warm spring Sunday morning that the boys ducked out at the end of that Sunday School class. Most of them were able to get home and change their clothes to some that were rough and rugged.

The boys had made a parachute just big enough for a big old tom cat. The harness was tom cat size, too. Sunday morning was the only time they could give the chute an honest to goodness live test. They would sneak into the grain elevator and two boys would ride the man lift to the top of the building.

Prowler was wearing the parachute harness, not with any pride. In fact it was not his idea at all. He was chucked out the window. The plan was that he would have so many feet of free fall, then the chute would open and the cat would float to the ground like a big winter snowflake.

The tom cat was still in the free fall mode when the parachute caught on a projecting piece of tin. The building was clad with galvanized tin panels, and one of these had a loose corner. Prowler complained loudly.

Church service would last no more than another hour. A speedy rescue was essential. Only two items were necessary, a wool blanket and a .22 caliber rifle.

Joey had a rifle and Pete could get the blanket. In a flash these two were back at the scene where the cat may die of starvation, and the boys well knew what they would be in for.

The gang of boys stood shoulder to shoulder and held on to the edge of the blanket. It was stretched into a rectangle that would fit a bed. Today, the blanket was an emergency landing pad for Prowler.

Joey aimed at the fine bit of line between the harness and the homemade parachute. It was a difficult shot because the string was only a few inches long and it was near the top of the building. Shooting up at an eighty degree angle was tough. He had brought a full box of shells for the rifle, which was a far sighted thing to do. At each shot the boys would tense up and pull the blanket tight. At each shot Prowler would count his remaining lives in case Joey wavered too much.

There were not too many of the box of fifty shells left when one connected. Down came Prowler. Instead of the red woolen landing pad Prowler picked Tim's shoulders with claws on all four feet extended to grip whatever he could to save his fall. This led to many fine parallel lines that turned into white scars on Tim's back. The lines stopped at his waist but it was a secret that the cat had pretty well tore Tim's pants off, too.

A few days later, the wind blew the mysterious rag off the side of the elevator.

Down the Creek

Henry Ford started making Model T Fords in 1907. That was the first one. The last one was in 1927. In all of that time the only changes were to the headlights, emblems and other decorations. Henry did not go for a lot of frills. The engine, transmission, and drive train were very much the same for the entire life of the T Ford.

The transmission was an early day marvel. It was controlled by two pedals at the driver's feet. Oh, there was a third pedal but it was for the brakes. When the driver pushed down the pedal on the left, the car was in first gear. There was a leaver on the left side of the driver, when it was moved forward and the pedal released the car would be in high gear. Jerk the lever back and step on the right pedal and there was reverse. The center pedal was for the brake. A person with big feet and in a rush may step on the center and right pedal at the same time. That made for a stop as well as reverse. That little maneuver was sure going to stop forward motion of the car.

In time even the very newest Model T Fords were getting pretty shaky. Martin put his old Ford to rest behind a granary. He bought an International One Ton truck from Mr. Hardman, the blacksmith and International Equipment dealer. That was about 1940.

In the early days there must have been a bad mud hole on the road allowance near the creek. The road made a grand curve and came to the creek at an angle so the bridge was built on that same angle. The bridge builders did not know Martin or give him a little tinkle of consideration.

The new truck had a big long shift leaver on the right side but nothing on the left like his Ford had. Very cautiously Martin drove around the curve, crossed the bridge and proceeded up the hill. The farther he got the harder the engine had to work. It was time for a lower gear. He stepped on the left pedal and reached for the high gear leaver with his left hand. There was no leaver, and stomp as he would, there was no low gear. He became somewhat unhinged as the truck picked up speed in reverse. He bravely held the left pedal down and missed the bridge and went over the bank and into the creek.

A few days ago I phoned my brother-in-law Norman.

"Say, Norman, do you know how they got Martin's new truck out of the creek?"

"I suppose they used a couple of tractors but I don't really know. But I was by there the other day and the truck was not there."

I had to chuckle to myself. I suppose that it did not take them sixty one years to get the truck back up over the creek bank. That was how long ago Martin washed his truck with a big splash.

The New Job

As the temporary shop foreman I felt that it was my duty to be helpful and friendly to customers. Oh sure, I lost some and gained some, but the losses were smaller than the gains.

It was a nice balmy spring day. The customer drove in with a year old Chevrolet station wagon.

"A rear wheel on my car has split. Can you do anything to help me?" This question came from the driver of the car with the Ohio license plate.

"I have never encountered a problem like that. It would be against the law to repair your wheel. The only hope would be a new wheel," I assured the gentleman.

It was only a minute or two and I asked the parts man, "Have we a wheel for a 1967 Chev?"

Another blink or two and I had the wheel at the paint shop door. John Wiebe was the prep. man. His job was to sand whatever and get it ready for paint. Real quick Glen Falk had the wheel painted. I carried the wheel to the tire department to have the Ohio tire mounted. Then Bud Armstrong called .

"Station wagons take a different wheel than passenger cars."

"Do we have a wagon wheel here?" I asked.

"Right here," Bud handed me the wheel.

"Hey, guys, guess what? I had you paint the wrong wheel. Do this one." Then to find the customer and tell him the truth without alibis.

"Oh, that is good that you are able to correct the little error. Will we still be able to drive to Calgary today?"

"It will be about a six hour drive. You should be there about dark," I assured him.

While the second wheel was being painted, he asked me a lot of questions. The tire was finally mounted and the wheel was put in its storage hole. I took a scrap of cardboard box and lay over the tire so dust would not fall on the fresh paint. I had just closed the rear door on his wagon and expected him to zoom away. Instead he said,

"My brother had a Chevrolet garage in Eureka, California. He should have you on his staff. I will give you a return air ticket for you and your wife if you will fly down and see the dealership and the city. I am sure you would enjoy working there."

Well, an offer like that was so big and so sudden that it nearly knocked my socks off. I phoned Berniece and it did the same to her socks. We did not even go.

Winter came and so did the oil man's burned out Pontiac. We had to scrub every inch of the interior. In was thick with soot.

The Big Oil Man from Oklahoma that had rented the car for a year, explained it all.

"I heard that the Oil Man's Bonspiel was on in Regina. I did not know what a bonspiel was but I figured that it would be fun and then I would represent our company. After the last game I stopped in front of the Hotel Saskatchewan. I left the car at the curb, and went in to see about my bill. Some one said that there was a car on fire out on the street. When I got through at the desk, I went back to my car.

It was my car that was burning. The firemen had all four doors open and they poured a million gallons of water into it. Them buggers had no mercy on anything."

That Dad Blamed Pontiac smelled like a burning barrel. Every thing we tried seemed so hopeful when we closed the doors on the car. It smelled good. In the morning the black burnt smell was still there and as strong as ever.

Bud had an idea! "There is a new aerosol spray out that is a cleaner and a disinfectant. We should try that."

"Good. Get us a half a dozen cans of it. We may have to drownd the Pontiac in it."

We sprayed a can on the interior of the car. At quiting time that tan car smelled like an operating room at the hospital. In the morning it smelled burnt.

The oil man took his car. He was able to cope by having the heater on high, his window down and a cigar in his teeth. That cigar was always burning. His relief came as a call back to head office in Oklahoma. The rough necks got the Pontiac to drive for the rest of the lease agreement. If I remember right, something bad happened to the Pontiac. We never saw it again.

The marvelous spray! What was it good for? We still had five cans of it. That was great.

A customer came with his Buick.

"My wife is a heavy smoker. My windshield is so clouded up that I think I need a new one."

I checked the glass and it was in top condition. I had a brain wave.

"We have some anti tobacco spray. I feel that it is no good, but if you will let me try it on your car it will not cost you a cent but there is no guarantee, of course. If it does not help we can put in a new windshield the next time that you are in town."

The customer went down town, and I cleaned the windshield inside and out. It sparkled. The ash tray got cleaned. It did not sparkle but it sure did have a different odor.

The Buick man promised to let me know if it worked or not. There were two Buicks and one Pontiac our garage had sold in that corner of our trading area. I did not see the man again during the rest of the winter.

A week later a fellow with a Ford car stopped in front of the garage. He was not a regular customer and seemed rather hesitant to even talk. Finally he asked about the anti tobacco spray. This had me off balance for a second or two. Then I remembered the line I had spieled out for the Buick owner.

"Oh yes, we have the stuff but it is just experimental. I don't think that it is any good but if you will let me, I'll try some on your car."

It was another case of cleaning a windshield, inside and out. I had asked to have the car for two hours. He came back at the agreed time, said thank you and drove away.

I must have cleaned a half a dozen cars from that district in the early part of that winter. We did not earn one blessed nickel, but we did get rid of one more can of disinfectant cleaner.

After the new year three of the guys that had smoky windshields came up with insurance claims and asked, "Will you fix my car?" That added a few thousand dollars to the body shop cash income.

One day the Ford body shop manager happened into our shop. When he saw three of his customer's cars at our place, he was somewhat riled up.

"Oh, they just came and asked if we could fix them and I said yes."

John McDaid, the president of the company, said, "That is bordering on fraud, but I'm glad you are for us and not against us."

Some Luck

Norma and Berniece were clearing away the dishes after a gigantic meal. Norma must have considered us as company, and she sure treats company royally. Walt and I sat at the dining room table so we would be on hand to play some crazy kind of a card game.

"Another time Joe and Bud and I were going hunting. We were going to take five horses in Joe's truck. The camp stuff would fit in my half ton truck. We were all riled up to go when Joe called and said that he just got a hauling job and said that he had to go to work."

Well, we thought it over. It seemed that our hunt had gone to the dogs.

Bud said, "Let's take your truck. We only need our saddle horses and two pack horses, and we can cut down on the camp stuff so it will all go in your truck."

"But my 1933 International hasn't been fit for the road for a long time. There are no clearance lights, no brake lights, no horn, no door handle on one side, and no licence. If we got caught, it would be bad for us."

"Tell you what! Let's get your truck ready and if we get caught, we'll split the fine," Bud offered.

Well, I got jacks and wrenches, the tire pump, lots of tire patches, and rolls of friction tape. I took everything the old truck might need, and nearly took the kitchen sink.

Then we had to go to Morningside. That is way up the highway from here at Penhold. We loaded Bud's horse and the two pack horses, but then had to come back down the highway here for my horse. The horses were in front, and we built a place for our camp things at the back. At last we were on the road past Sylvan Lake, Rocky Mountain House, and down the Forestry Trunk road. We were across the North Ram River when we had a flat tire on the right front.

We got the tube patched and I was pumping away. It takes a lot of strokes up and down to fill a truck tire. Bud sounded like he was choking, "Walt, a cop is stopping here."

"I wished that I was home right about then."

Norma walked by the table and with the attitude of every sport hunter's wife the world over. She said, "You both should have stayed home, you old fools."

Walt continued, " The cop wasn't ugly but he was pretty much for business."

"Who owns the truck,?" was his first question.

"It's mine." I spoke right up.

"Where is your licence plate?" That was the second question and it seemed they were getting harder as he went along.

Bud was getting some upset, "Hey Walt, you lost the licence plate and you lost the horn, too."

The officer was writing down my driver licence number when Bud shouted, "Your car is on fire." I grabbed my gauntlet gloves and ran and opened the hood on the police car. There was a big chunk of foam rubber shoved down beside the manifold. It had just started to burn. I threw it out on the ground, and put dirt on the burning wires. I got the car fire out. The cop got the grass fire out that the burning rubber started. Bud came puffing up with a pail of water from the river. He had a good idea but he was too late with his effort.

The Nordegg mines were going then. While I was taping up the wires that had their insulation burned off, the cop started to unload his troubles on us if we cared to listen.

"Them miners at Nordegg are out to get me. I have never so much as gave a ticket to anyone there. That don't matter to them guys. They do every thing possible to embarrass or even kill me. This foam rubber trick was the latest of their fun and games."

I had the wires taped up so I said, "Try it." The car started and seemed to run as good as ever. The cop stuck his head out the window and said, "Thanks, boys, have a good hunt. " Then he drove away.

I said to Bud, "You should not have told him that we lost the horn, too. It is under the truck seat."

The Red Truck

It was forty-nine years after the fact that Jerry and Wally met again and found their memories amusing.

Jerry Doll and Walter Ceislak had worked in a mine near Princeton B.C.. Three years of mining were behind them. They boarded the Greyhound Bus for Vancouver early that morning.

Every few miles Jerry would take his money out of his shirt pocket and count it. The final figure was the same every time, nineteen hundred and seven dollars. It was a heady feeling to have that much cash. Jobs were hard to find and many young fellas were close to going hungry. Here was a guy twenty-two years old with a hard earned fortune in his shirt pocket. He counted it again, and it was still nineteen hundred and seven dollars.

The purpose of the trip was to buy a new car or truck for a trip home to Saskatchewan.

"You know, Jerry, if you run short of money, I am here to help." Wally was a good friend to make such an offer.

Dueck Motors on Hastings Street sure looked like a good place to start hunting for a vehicle. It was about 8:30 in the morning and the Chevrolet show room was just waking up.

"Good Morning, boys. Is there something I can do for you?" the salesman asked. His manner just made you know that he would be a good friend to have.

"Yes, I want to buy a car or truck," Jerry told him.

"You boys are in luck today. We have a large selection of very nice used units on the side lot. Just come this way." The new found friend was ready to guide them out to see all of the prize junk in the far back row.

"No, I want something new," Jerry claimed. "How much is this coupe?"

"That car is a 2-10-27. That is the top of the line of our Chev coupe models. The basic price is about nineteen hundred dollars. With the additional features it will cost well over that figure."

Moving away from the gold mine priced car, and over by the side door, stood a red truck.

"This is a nice looking truck. How much will it cost me?"Jerry asked.

"The bare bones price on this unit is sixteen hundred and twelve dollars. Then we have to add the cost of the exterior sun visor, cab corner windows, whitewall tires, heater, rear view mirror and the spare wheel and tire. These items add two hundred and seventy three dollars to the base price."

"Good. I'll take it,"Jerry announced.

The salesman was shocked out of his early morning politeness.

"Please come into my office and we can get the deal fixed up."

The man was behind his desk, Jerry right across and Wally had a chair to one side.

"What finance company or bank do you hope to get the money from to pay for the truck?"

Jerry said, "I'll pay cash." He edged closer to the desk, reached into his shirt pocket for the money and peeled off eighteen hundred and eighty five dollars and handed it across the desk.

"Excuse me for just a minute." The salesman scooped up the money and left the office.

"We sure are lucky. It is not even nine o'clock and you have a new truck," Wally observed.

The salesman was back behind his desk. He shuffled around in the desk to find a sales contract that would do for the deal on the red truck.

With his pen poised he asked ,"What is your name?"

"Jerry Doll."

"Is that all, no middle name or initial?"

"I am Jerome Isidore Doll if it makes a difference to that piece of paper." Jerry was happy and joking. He had just bought a new truck.

The salesman wrote on the form and again excused himself from the office. After a long wait he returned with the sales contract but the money was elsewhere.

"Jerry, where do you work?"

"Oh, I'm between jobs right now."

The guy took off again.

The boys sat and waited. It was now after ten.

"Jerry, if money is a problem I'll sure help out," Wally offered.

The salesman came back, sat in his chair and asked, "Where do you live, Jerry?"

"Oh, as soon as I get the truck I think we will head for Saskatchewan."

The salesman had to take himself to another office. He was gone for most of an hour.

"Jerry, if money is the hold up I'll help," Wally offered.

The salesman returned. "Sorry boys, this is taking a long time." He was gone again.

It was passed the noon hour when the boys got up and were walking out of the building. They had not had food since they had joined the early shift of miners at the cook shack. All of a sudden there seemed to be people that were very interested in the boys whereabouts and welfare.

"Don't go away boys. We will soon have everything all straightened out."

"You bet we won't go away. You still have my money somewhere," Jerry answered.

After lunch they were back at Dueck Motors.

The salesman met them at the door. "Oh good, you are back. I thought for a while we had lost you."

"Is my truck ready?" Jerry wanted to know.

"Not yet but it will be ready soon."

The boys had to wait.

"Jerry, if it's money, I will give you some." Wally still held out a hand.

By four-thirty the boys had looked at every car and truck in the show room, they had read every poster on the walls, and sat on every padded bench in the place. More than once they stopped to have a look at the red five window Chev. "Imagine that, white wall tires on a truck."

The sales staff must have been in a big sweat trying to find where the two guys had done a robbery and wanted a truck to go to Saskatchewan with. They had been on the phone to the cops in Canada and the U.S.A. since before nine that morning.

The gent that the boys had spotted as a plain clothes RCMP officer had been in and out of the salesmen's office off and on and had come to take a sly look at the boys.

Wally wondered, "Do you suppose they stole the red truck and that is the problem? Or, maybe the guy that bought your log cabin gave you counterfeit money?"

The light donned on Jerry. "They are checking to see where we stole the money."

The salesman was at his desk. Jerry went into the office and handed his wallet to the man.

"There is my driver's licence, and here are my last two pay stubs. I cashed the cheques yesterday. And, I sold my cabin near the mine because we are leaving there."

The salesman took the wallet to another office and was back in ten minutes.

"Please sign here, and here are the keys for your new truck."

Soon Jerry and Wally were driving down the street in the new Red Truck. Oh, it was a beauty. They had not gone very far when they drove past a theater.

"After sitting around that garage all day, I think we should treat ourselves to a movie." Jerry suggested.

Wally agreed, and Jerry pulled over to the curb and parked the new Red Truck.

After the show or about two hours later, they came back to the truck. There was no truck. The new Red Truck was gone.

A city policeman on his beat was nearby. Jerry approached him in a somewhat agitated frame of mind.

"My new Red Truck is gone and here are the keys. I've had them in my pocket all the time."

"Where did you park your truck?" the policeman asked.

"Right here. Right by this sign. Here is where we parked two hours ago." Jerry was still short his new Red Truck.

The officer explained. "This is a no parking zone. Your truck has been towed to the city police compound."

It was at the police station where the charge was forty dollars. Then Wally's money came into play.

Too Little To Smoke

It was them Muri boys again! Only this time it was the next generation. The original pioneers, Ben Nybo and Andrew Muri, located their homes a half a mile apart. The Muri farmyard was on the west side of a deep coulee. There were small branch coulees and one of these ended on level ground not far from the Nybo yard.

The neighborhood gathering was at Nybos that Sunday. There was a yard full of cars. It was no problem to search through them until they found cigarettes. Two Muri guys, Ivan and Duane and their cousin Ron took the smokes and walked across the coulee to the Muri home.

Grandpa Muri was at home. When he heard three grandchildren in the kitchen, moving a chair so they could climb up to the match box holder, he became very suspicious. The chair was left in a position that no adult would have sat on. He peeked out the window. There were the three fellows walking to the barn. They were walking away, with their backs to Grandpa's view. Front or back, Grandpa knew guilt when he saw it. The boys went into the barn.

Grandpa put on his cap, and took his mountain staff in his hand. (He was young when he left Norway but he still remembered the six foot long canes the old men had at that time. He had one of his own now). He went to the barn.

The young grandsons were not so dumb either. One of them had an eye to a crack in the wall.

"Here comes Grandpa. We better get out of here quick." They did a little sneak maneuver and were out of sight in the coulee.

Grandpa stood out by the barn and waved his long cane. Uncle Sidney saw the signal, got in his car and sped up the road to home. He and grandpa inspected the barn but found nothing out of the ordinary. Before he was back at Nybos, the three boys had emerged from the coulee and mixed right in the gathering.

The unlit cigarettes had been put down a gopher hole. There was no smell and no evidence, so what could go wrong.

Uncle Sidney interrogated the three guys. No, they had not been smoking in the barn. They stuck to their guns on that. That was the sum and total of the smoking trip.

I asked Dr.Philp Muri D.M.V. if he thought that I should write about that episode.

"Of course you should. At that time I was too little to smoke."

No Got

What a night! It really started at three o'clock that Saturday afternoon. We were living in Lethbridge, Alberta. I was an auto body man at Enerson Motors. Berniece and the kids were visiting in Saskatchewan. It was a lonesome afternoon. To kill time I went down to see our friends at the Christensen Funeral Parlor.

Cecal Fleming, the vice president, John Hockstra, the man that did the work, and myself were sitting having coffee in the staff room.

"I don't think too much of the guys you work for," Cec said.

"Had trouble with them?" I asked.

"No, but they cannot fix the back door on the Pontiac Ambulance."

"What is wrong with it?" I asked.

"It binds and will not close smooth. I have taken it back there time and again. They can't seem to adjust it right."

John piped in, "You have had it to every other body shop in the city, and they have done nothing for it either."

Tipping up the last drop of coffee, I said, "Lets go and see that terrible Pontiac."

We had just acquired a new Pontiac, and were proud of it.

"John, you take him up to the garage. The keys are on the board in the office." Cec was not going to inspect that door again.

We opened the door and John closed it again. It was not good.

After many looks and checks, I spotted a bright bit of sunlight reflected on the lower door hinge. There should have been paint there and nothing shiny. We took that part off the car. Sure enough, it was a factory flaw. It had to have more clearance. I filed for a while, John filed for a while, and then it was my turn again. We finally got enough metal cut away. Everything was put together. The back door of the ambulance closed like a fridge door.

"Come back and have a chicken supper with us," John invited.

"Good, I'll have a shower and change, and be right back."

It was about five-thirty when I parked behind the funeral home. Melvin Christensen opened the garage door.

"Oh, please don't park there. I have to gas up the Pontiac."

So I moved over and parked by the Buick hearse door. I leisurely went up the stairs to the apartment. John was holding the phone.

"Will you take an ambulance run for me tonight?"

"Why, of course." I had fixed so many cars that had been in highway wrecks, so I may as well see what it is like at the scene.

"Joan is down in the office doing up some forms for the trip. There is chicken on the stove. Help yourself, and then get down to the garage." Then he talked to someone on the other end of the line.

I grabbed a small drumstick, and chewed on it on the way to the garage. There was Melvin back with the Pontiac.

"So you are my spare driver for tonight."

"I guess so," was my lame reply. Somehow this did not sound like we were going to scrape someone off the highway a few miles out of town.

I got in and Melvin wheeled the vehicle around to the RCMP building. Out came a Mountie with two women. Melvin said, "Get the side door open, and the jump seats down." I jumped right at it. The ladies got in, and we drove away.

West out of the city! What gives here, I wondered? Across the bridge and up the hill, I got the first hint of what was ahead.

"We are taking a patient to the hospital at Ponoka," Melvin said. He must have figured that was enough for me to know.

Near Calgary one lady asked the other if she was hungry. The answer was, "No." Melvin gave the same answer.

"Good, we will go right on then," she said.

This seemed strange. Melvin was driving, but the gal on the front jump seat was calling the shots. Oh well, it's all right I suppose.

We had just crossed 16 Ave. N. in Calgary. Melvin announced, 'It's your turn to drive."

Sure enough. I had gone a mile when we came upon road construction. Number 2 was getting a major face lift, and it started to rain. The gal in the back advised me to take it easy. It was after midnight when they coached me on finding the way to the hospital admitting door.

We were met by a nurse who opened the doors for us. Such courtesy. After going though about six doors, we were in the admitting office. There the lady who had taken charge of our voyage, handed over some official papers. Ann, it seemed, had come to the end of her trip. She was left at the hospital.

I felt like fresh air would suit me about then. I got up to go, but the door was locked.

Ann, with a voice as from another world, said, "You do not go through doors here. They are locked."

About then I realized I was in an institution for people that had not taken good care of all their marbles.

Back in the car, with Melvin driving, the boss lady said, "Stop in Red Deer for a coffee."

At a late closing spot on Gatze Avenue, we did learn that our fellow traveler was Elsie.

"Are you boys hungry?" she asked.

I remembered the drumstick of eight or nine hours ago, "Yes, I believe I could use a snack."

"And you, Mr. Christensen," this was aimed at Melvin.

He said, "Yes."

She said , "Good ," then to the waitress, "Bring us three coffee and three doughnuts. If you eat much it will be harder to stay awake.

That is all you guys can have now. It is getting late, and we have a long drive."

Back in the Pontiac, she requested , "Make out the stretcher and lock it down." Lying down on the thing, she asked for a blanket. With that tucked around her, she added, "Put two safety belts on me and wheel this thing home. If we are stopped, don't say a word, I'll do the talking. I am a special RCMP constable. Oh yes, stop at Claresholm."

Melvin wheeled it. It was not long and we were in Calgary. At 16 Ave, he stopped. "Now it is your turn again."

I was scooting along 4 St. (that was before Calgary used the MacLeod Trail). Melvin bet that I could not make the green traffic light. I did. This went on light after light. We were nearly out of the city, and I was still going through green lights. Two blocks ahead a car came from the right, and it entered our street without stopping. Where the police cruiser came from, we don't know. It sure pulled over the stop signs runner, and they waved us on with their flashlight.

We had the top alternating lights on, and in a panic Melvin said to push the siren just enough so it would growl. That I did. You see I was driving twice the speed limit, to get through those green lights.

My heartbeat was normal when we went through Okotoks. It was day light then.

I stopped the car at Claresholm as requested. The police lady was released from the stretcher. She claimed that she had slept for most of the time. We just left it the way it was. It could be put away later. At that time of day there was no place open in town, so we drove on. Our police constable sat in front with Melvin and I.

"It is a pity that we had to make this trip. That girl was not in danger. Her husband could have taken her to the hospital. Their Indian beet workers had hid a gallon of home brew on the farm. She found it, and in one drink, her mind was gone. She will be home again in a couple of months."

After divulging that information, Elsie cast off her police role. She was a motherly type person.

"I retired from nursing two years ago, and I think, I will also turn in my RCMP badge and papers, and call this my last trip. It was nearly fifty years ago that I got my nurse's cap. About half that long I have been riding in ambulances, ever since the Mounties figured they needed a guard with medical knowledge.

I was pushing the gas pedal quite hard, and we were going south rather fast. She gazed west towards the Porcupines.

"When my father came from England, he homesteaded out there. I was the youngest of three girls. One time we went to a school house dance. A bunch of us young people traveled in a bob sleigh with a team of horses. It was bitter cold, but we had robes and horse blankets over us to keep warm.

At one place the sleigh road was at the edge of a steep bank of the North Fork of the Oldman River. Our driver did something wrong. We all rolled down the bank to the ice on the river.

In those days girls wore tight waisted dresses, and seven petticoats. By the time you have rolled forty feet in soft snow, the seven under garments are loaded with the cold white stuff. Thank Goodness for the tight waist. We were not wet above there.

There was no way to dry our clothes. A girl would die of mortification before she would admit that her underclothes were wet.

We got to the dance, and did we dance! It was a high old time that kept on until daylight. We were so warmed up from the dancing. Then we put our coats on. The drive home was horrible. When we got home, there was ice at the hem of my dress, and some on the petticoats.

The next day my mouth and gums, well all of my face ached.

Mother said, "She has Neuralgia."I was given three aspirin tablets, and told to rest.

Father said, "She needs a cop o' Hoodsen Bayy Room."

This cure all of father's was bought at the Hudson Bay store at Fort Macleod for twenty-five or fifty cents a gallon. You had to take in your own empty jug. It was like thick molasses. It was strange! A spoon full of hot water mixed in a cup of that stuff would turn it to liquid. A spoon full of that rum in a glass of water would make one of today's highballs. It was the original Hudson Bay Rum, the same as the fur traders used.

Father came with such a cup, "Drink this."

I sat up in bed and swallowed the whole cupful of that awful stuff.

Father said, "Now sleep," which I did for two days.

Elsie's story had been punctuated by many smirks and giggles.

Then she said, "I slept for two days and was drunk for another one, and I haven't taken a drink since. This brought on a riot of laughter.

She dried her eyes, "My heavens, I'm getting giddy," and she shook with laughter.

The Greyhound bus depot was open at Fort MacLoed. We had a very quiet and sedate coffee break.

Thirty miles to go. Back in the Pontiac, it was our turn to laugh and hoot. For the rest of the trip Elsie was better than most comedians.

I was directed to Elsie's house. I stopped the ambulance at her door. Before she got out there was another peel of laughter.

"We should drive down the street a few yards. Then you boys could take me by each an arm, while I stagger to the house. Boy, that would get the neighbours' tongues on fire." Another laugh and she donned her police mantel. With a Goodnight she sedately walked to her front door.

Goodnight! It was nearly eight o'clock Sunday morning. Melvin unlocked the garage door, and I drove the Pontiac in where it usually stayed. Melvin had disappeared. It had been twenty-six hours since I had been in bed. That is where I went.

It was a few months later, and Melvin was home for the weekend. He had a good job in Calgary, but spent many off hours at home with his folks. His father Chris had a serious heart condition so Melvin spent as much time with him as he could.

On Sunday afternoon, at four-thirty, the phone rang.

"This is Chris calling. Cec and John are both away on a case. Could you come and help us?"

"Yes, I will be right down."

Melvin had the Pontiac out and was behind the wheel. This trip took us to the General Hospital. With a bit of coaching on Melvin's part I was able to help him move the old man's body from the hospital bed to the marble table at the funeral home.

We had the stretcher folded and ready to put back in the ambulance when Chris met us.

"Boys, there was an Indian drowned at Cardston on Thursday. They just found him today. You have to go and pick him up."

I asked, "You have a man at Cardston?"

Chris answered, "Yes, it was our agent there that called in."

Melvin looked at his watch and said, "Good, we will be home by seven-thirty."

I answered him, "I will beat that. I'll be home in ten minutes."

That was the end of my career with the undertakers. They just never called me again.

Monday morning at the body shop, as we were getting into our coveralls to start work, I mentioned my activity of the two days before.

Big blue-eyed John Carlson from Denmark, who had recently joined our staff, told me what he thought.

"Bernie, as a undertooker you yust don't got it."

Harry Bill

The sign on the side of the building proclaimed it as Christenson's Auto Body Shop. It was a small business run by myself and some times five employees. Besides dent straightening and painting, we had many customers that would order mechanical parts to install on their own vehicles.

There were people that would come and have us order parts and not be able to pay for them. Harry Bill came in July and ordered parts for his four wheel drive truck. These pieces were for the steering system of the truck. The parts came but Harry did not. He came at Christmas time and asked about his order.

"Yes, your parts are here," I told him.

"I can't take them today but keep them for me. I have my skidder and a crew working down in the Cypress Hills. We will be logging there for the rest of the winter."

The Cypress Hills are in the southwest corner of Saskatchewan and that meant that Harry was working four hundred miles away from home. I realized that the cost of moving his big machine that far and paying his helpers would take a lot of money.

In January Harry was back just for a short visit one day.

"The contractor paid us all up by cheque in the evening. In the morning I went to the bank in Maple Creek. There I found out that I had a problem. He had taken every thing in cash and had closed out his account the afternoon the day before. Everyone that he had charge accounts with was stuck with bad cheques. He and his wife drove away during the night. No one had any idea where they could be found. When I looked at my cheque for several thousand dollars, I could have shot him. I would have had to be the first one to find him, there were other people ready to kill him, too. Now I will be flat broke by the time I get my skidder home," Harry said.

If the contractor that skipped with the money would have come face to face with this tall muscular Indian he would not have survived. I felt sorry for Harry.

One morning near the end of March we found that there had been a light snow fall during the night. That afternoon Harry came to the shop. He was in a much better frame of mind than the last time I had seen him.

"How much is my bill?" he asked.

I looked in old sales books from the year before and found one. Harry Bill, Chitek Reserve, truck parts, eighty-nine dollars and thirty cents. "Here it is," I handed him the bill.

"Good, I'll take them today." And he handed me the money.

"Yesterday a couple of guys came out to collect a payment on my hay baler. Well, they were out of luck. I did not have money enough for groceries. They were kind of definite, too, money or the baler. There were two of them in a car. They told me that they would be back today with a truck with a bumper hitch so that they could pull the baler back to where ever they take balers that they steal from Indians.

Last night when it started to snow I had my brother Alfred help me. We took the baler across a swamp and parked it in a stand of heavy spruce trees. With the snow covering our tracks I knew that they would never find the baler.

This morning I saw them coming and I drove out the back road. I had to wait until they were in my driveway so I would not meet them on the highway. If there was no cheque in the mail, I would be harder to find than the baler. I had told my wife to tell them that I had just gone to town for the mail, and I would be right home again.

I had done miles of cut lines for Sask Power and they were slow at paying. This morning there was a cheque from them for over three thousand dollars. I cashed it and drove like crazy to get back home. I asked the fellas what could I do for them? They didn't even want to talk to me. They just wanted the baler and to get going down the road. I got them in and sat at the table with a cup of coffee. I asked if they would consider getting enough money to cover all but the last payment that is not due for two years. They sure had a fast change in attitude. Now as soon as you find my parts, I had better go and get my baler home before the swamp starts to thaw out."

Black Spark

If I had only paid more attention when Simon was telling me about Treaty Number Seven.

I will not try to write as Simon told the story. He learned to speak English at the sanatorium where he overcame tuberculosis. He was not a highly educated person but he had the dignity like the first fur traders found in the Indians. They were equal to anyone and honest.

"We should have shared the land with the white men instead of selling it."

"The man that said he was from the Great White mother was not good warrior.If he had been an Indian, he would have been left at home with the women. He would never have shot a buffalo. He would have been skinning the game and carrying the meat home."

"It happened a long time ago, when the old men were kids and they heard the story from old men who lived then. When we were kids they told us."

"The sun has all of the power. It gives power to the earth. The earth gives the Indian power with animals and fish and berries and all of that food."

"The white man did not want to buy our sun, he knew that he could not get it. He wanted our land. That would break the chain of power and the Indians would be hungry or have to beg for food from the white men. We Indians can not take power from the sun without the land."

"The men came from the Queen in England. They wanted to buy our land. They said that they would feed us and give us five dollars cash every year. Some of the Chiefs said that was a good deal because some years there were no buffalo or any animals, and then the people starved."

"Most of the people said no. If we give up the land we lose our power to live. The food the white man will give us is not Indian food. It will make us sick."

"The Chiefs went to a camp close to Fort Carlton. There they signed away our land."

"A young man went hunting. He was not right in the head. In a dream he learned that he should hunt for a black mark and shoot it. His father was one Chief that signed at the camp with the white men. He dreamed to take a black spark from the cold fire and with the stick make X on his forehead. He sat by the cold fire and thought about the treaty. In the morning his son came home. He saw the black spark so shot an arrow. The arrow killed the Chief because he signed the treaty."

Bits from Here and There

Little lumps of knowledge:

At this point in time------ means that the speaker doesn't know what the heck time it is now. He got the watch for a present, and has not learned it's use, or how to use it.

I am ---------------------not withstanding, means he don't know what he is talking about and is not sure if he is really standing or sitting.

I will have you know---------- means that the speaker doesn't know any thing, but is willing to share his knowledge.

To this day ----- What a night he had!

But note this------ write it down. He may forget what he is talking about.

A piece of my mind-------- it will have to be a very small piece, because there is not very much there to share in the first place.

If a rattle snake kills a gopher for his lunch, don't sympathize with the gopher.

The sign says Tasty Bagels, but are they friendly to dentures.

If you wait till tomorrow, the hill that you have to climb will be just as high as it was yesterday.

If the sun does not rise in the east, you may be on the wrong street.

Before the cake is served , put away the cookbook.

If you have a tough job on hand, give it to the laziest staff member. Then watch it being done the easiest way possible.

If you see the white heads at church, it is not ripe dandelions. It's seniors.

Lonesome Dog

It was somewhere between Spiritwood and Leoville that this happened and I cannot remember who told me about it. Seventy five years ago people from Quebec, New Brunswick, Vermont, Ontario and Saskatchewan started settling on the flat forest land in north central Saskatchewan. Life had not been perfect at the old home place so they set out to have a better life on homesteads.

Jules Chalifour said that he was told that there were roots and rocks on the land near Leoville.

"We had roots in Quebec and I met rocks at Vonda. But I did not know that at Leoville there was a rock under every root."

Some of the new farmers had some money, many were going only on hope. One thing most folks had in common was that they were of French decent.

At the new home a shelter or dwelling of some sort was the first on the list of things that had to be done. The second was a well. Either dig a well or carry water from the neighbours or the river. A person has to have a drink of water while chopping down trees to make a field, and it is nice to have a wash or a bath once in a while.

With one family the house and garden were in place and the well was dug.

That well was a godsend, clear cold water and a never failing amount. The well was such a treasure that the farmer built a dog wheel to pump water. The thing was patterned like a water wheel so common in Quebec but it was not powered by a waterfall or fast flowing stream. It was dog power that run the thing. The wheel was about eighteen inches wide with the sides boarded in. The pooch would go in the little door in the side of the wheel and trot. As the dog moved forward his weight would move the wheel. While the dog trotted along the wheel would turn so the animal stayed at the bottom of the wheel. There was some kind of a hookup from the wheel to the pump handle.

When a person went for a pail of water he would whistle for the dog and hang the pail on the pump spout. That furry friend would go in the door on the side of the wheel and start his dog trot and the wheel would start turning. In a minute or two the water pail would be full and the dog's job was done.

On a bright morning the good folks walked to Sunday Mass.

After church they were invited to have dinner with friends. The meal was delicious and the conversation good. It was so good that it was near sundown when the folks got back home. The whole farmyard was ankle deep in mud. To fight boredom the dog had gone into his wheel and pumped water all day long. There was water everywhere.

The master put his hand on the dog's head, and said,

"Je vais barrer la porte, et de toi, mon amie, je vais cacher la clé."

I should lock the door, and from you my friend I will hide the key

First Request

It was more than a hundred years ago that the Hispanic family made their way into the mountains of New Mexico. The road from Santa Fe to Taos had been traveled for two hundred years. These people left the civilized world of the Jemez Indians. The trail north from Santa Fe went through their land. Jose and his wife guided their goats along the ridges of stone, into the mountains. They made their path by the edge of deep canyons. After miles of travel, they found the Pajarito Plateau. The spring fed lake proved to be the end of their search for a new home. This meadow , surrounded by sheltering mountains, had every requirement for their home and flock. Wood, water, grass and the protection of the mountains, and isolation was all they needed for the life style they chose.

Years went by, then a guide with a party of eastern gentlemen found the goat ranch. The eastern people were impressed with the beauty and solitude of the lake with its' hills and mountains, and it was many miles from anywhere. These men were the rich nation builders of the United States. Around their campfire they developed the plan to build a school at this site.

That evening was the seed that grew into The Ranch School For Boys. It was a school for <u>elite</u> boys. The youngsters would kick over the traces at home, they had money to spend. The fathers were too busy making more money, so time with their sons was limited.

In the late summer of 1917 a group of New York boys that had shown rangytang inclinations, traveled by Pullman coach to New Mexico. They were now out west, but no romantic stage coach was at the station for them. Their luggage was tossed into a wagon, and the boys sat on it. They spent the next two days on a wagon ride to their new school.

It was a Spartan type of education. At day break the boys were out of bed and went for a nude dip in the lake. I guess that was all right, if the girls from the goat ranch had promised not to peek.

This group of students spent from four to five years before they graduated. The last group spent three months, of morning dips, and then they graduated courtesy of Uncle Sam, who needed the school.

The United States was at war. There were three scientists working in three different basement suites, in an eastern city. Their job was to build the ultimate weapon that would be so powerful that it would end all wars. At the time there was a threat of foreign agents stealing the formulas.

A place was needed that would be secure, and easy to protect. A spot right in the middle of nowhere, free from all outside traffic was required.

What better place than the Ranch School for Boys. Out in New Mexico a spy would have a two day walk to get near the place. In the meantime he would look like a fly in a milk bottle. Uncle Sam said, "The students graduate before the end of February. We must have the school by March the first."

That was the beginning of the Lab, (U.S. Atomic Energy Laboratory, Los Alamos, New Mexico). It was such a well kept secret that the people that worked there were at P.O.box 15 U.S.A..

The branch of government that was responsible for the project found just the right man as boss over the Lab. He was one straight forward guy that wore an expensive Stetson hat. His office had a desk and chair, plus a little perch of a chair for Mary, the steno, when she was called in to take notes for a letter.

"Mary, send a request to the Property Maintenance boys. 'Pound a spike in the wall behind the desk in Director's office. It is needed to hang his hat on,' they should find time for that."

A day later.

"Mary send a note to Property Maintenance. 'Please remove ottoman from Directors office. He does not have to sit on it to put his boots on. Instal spike as in first request,' Now, that should do."

Another day later.

"Mary send a note to Maintenance. 'Come and remove hall tree. Director has only one hat. One spike as in first request will do.' Don't them guys know what a spike is?"

The next day.

"Mary take a note," ' Property Maintenance. The spike is just right. It works great. Thank You, sincerely.'

The Director.

Youth

The first year that we had that land, I was anxious to cut hay. There was a gently rolling sixty acre field of mixed hay ready to be cut. The haybine dealer claimed that the machine would work at eight miles an hour. The Case tractor had a gear that moved at that speed. That was the one I used. I hit a boulder that was sticking up six inches, and that broke a knife guard. There was only a couple of rocks like that I was told. Twenty rocks later I was finished.

The next year Leroy cut that field.

I was helping Eph McKellep get his baler back to the field. He had hit a few rocks with it. His son Bob was called to the Yukon to manage a diamond drill. He took Leroy with him.

"How are you coming with your hay?" Eph asked.

"All I have down is the field across from you. Tomorrow I will bale and stack it."

Some more pounding tin and he asked, "How did Lee make out with the haybine?

"Better than I did last year. I broke twenty guards. Lee broke two."

"How did he do it?" Eph asked.

"He slowed down about four gears so the machine had time to slide over the rocks," I explained,

Eph was seventy years old. He stared off into the distance. "We got to watch these kids. Sometimes they think for themselves."

Leroy and Cecil Grassic were short a subject in high school. This pair to be funny signed up for Home Economics. They each did sew an apron. Cooking skills? Maybe?

While we were making hay, our sons were way up north. From Whitehorse, Y.T they were on a smaller plane to the drill site. When Bob and Lee stepped off the plane, the cook and an injured man got on. Bob had worked for that company for possibly twenty years. This is the way he told me it was.

"I sent Leroy to man the cook tent. I was too busy to get him started on the drills. The first meal was hamburger and cream corn. The meat was over done and the corn had popped. The crew grumbled. The next day he made a stew - meat, vegetables and potatoes all in a big kettle. It smelled good. At last the men were looking forward to a meal. The dumb kid had drained off all the juice and we had to eat dry stew. Lee had just made a four layer chocolate cake, chocolate icing and all. Now that looked good, but the work gang were hinting of murder.

The next day the big boss flew in. He got out of his plane and settled the business that he had come for.

"How about a cup of coffee before I go?" the boss asked.

"Go to the cook tent, and good luck." The men smirked behind his back.

"Any coffee?" he wondered.

Lee set a cup of coffee in front of the boss. "Care for a piece of cake?"

"Yes if you have some."

Out came yesterday's cake. A plate and fork were set in front of the honored person. The fourth cup of coffee and at least half of the cake was gone when the President thanked Lee, and went to his plane.

The plane motors was turning over slowly in its warm up time.

The workers that were not out on the drills came running .

"When are we going to get a cook?" They shouted in unison.

The President poked his head out of the window and shouted back, "You guys don't know when you are well off."

He shoved the throttle ahead and Zoom he was on the beam to Whitehorse,Y.T.

I asked Leroy about the cooking job that lasted only a few days, until the cook got back.

His version differed from Bob's a little bit, but he did say,

"I have been in at least a hundred camps since then. There is always someone ready to kill the cook. I say, 'Yes, it is hard to have a good variety of food out in the wilderness.' And, I always thank and congratulate the cook."

Twister

Now that was a storm. It roared through in July 1938. It passed to the north of our farm, then made the turn south and then went straight east.

Basil Nybo and I were taking a team of horses to Uncle David. He was farming north east of Kelstern, Sk. We were riding Dolly and Charm, an in-between pair that were good for riding, but big enough for harness work.

We followed the neighborhood trail across the Fred Child's pasture with a gate on the west and east sides. That joined a wagon road across Sam Buttler's field, through his yard and out to the road. That short cut saved about three miles of travel. We jogged north for a ways and rode across Abe Tomlinson's grain field. Two days ago it had been a grain field. Now it was a devastated plot of land. There was the odd plant that had a straw standing four inches high, but they were far apart. The ground had some crop residue showing, but most of it had been driven into the soil by giant hail stones.

The havoc was even greater three and four miles east.

While we rode along, we saw the roof line of a house over the rise a half a mile to the south. The crop on that farm looked like a mighty poor job of summer fallowing rather than a crop of wheat.

Near Hodgeville the storm must have veered off to the south. There it showed no damage.

Years later I became acquainted with the people that lived in the house that we had seen the roof of in 1938. Mr. and Mrs. Doll with their family lived there.

Years later, early one morning, I boarded the train at Hallonquist. I was on my way to see a dentist in Moose Jaw. On the passenger coach was a pretty girl with a yellow lace shawl covering all but the front of her face. It was tied with the cutest little bow under her chin, which I thought was cute, too.

A couple of weeks later at a wedding dance in Hodgville, I was wandering around like a steer on poor pasture when I saw the girl that wore the yellow scarf. To most girls I was big and clumsy with unruly hair. I swallowed all thoughts of myself. The orchestra started playing and I went and asked this girl for a dance. She gave a tiny little smile and said, "Certainly." She was tall and slim, but I was just over the six foot mark with long arms, and dancing with girls was not my specialty. She stepped out to dance, and when she put an arm on my shoulder and I got my arm around her slender waist, I felt that I would never want to let her go. She just fit in my arm so nice. I learned that she was sent home on the train that morning from the convent where she was going to school in Swift Current. The nuns suspected she had mumps. Her name was Berniece Doll.

Time sped on. After a dance we were sitting in the car in Mr. Doll's yard. To get this girl to her door and say goodnight was the plan. There was a distant flash of lightning far to the southeast. For a second Berniece trembled.

"What is wrong?" I asked with some concern.

"It goes back to when I was a little girl." Then she went on to explain.

"It was in the summer of 1938. Dad was away, so were Florence and Norbert. Mom was home with the rest of us kids. In the evening the sky got very dark. Mom lit a candle and told us to pray. There was a terrible rush of wind and a crash that made the house shake. Then an awful scraping sound. That was followed by more wind and the pounding of large hail stones against our house. After the storm passed there was still a bit of daylight left so we went out to see what damage had been done. We found that the roof of the barn had been blown against the side of our house. The heavy beam my Grandfather had brought from Minnesota. It was eight inches square and as long as the barn and had supported the roof. It had been driven end ways by the wind and had missed the house by a small six inches. The barn was at least two hundred yards west of the house. The wind had been that terribly strong."

With the telling of the memory of that terrifying night, Berniece gave a sob and a shiver and threw her arms around my neck, hid her face on my shoulder and said, "I have no protection from storms. Nowhere do I feel safe." I had my right arm around that trim waist. She quickly regained her composure. We said Good Night.

It was fifty-nine years later practically to the day of the first storm that I finally learned how deeply that storm of long age had seared Berniece's mind.

Early on a Sunday morning in July, 1997, we took our Granddaughters, Lisa Mumm and Robyn Christenson, for a holiday trip to the Black Hills of South Dakota. We checked into the Ace Motel at Belle Fourche, and then went to the Passion Play at Spearfish, S.D.

The Passion Play depicts the life and death of Jesus Christ. At the end of the play there is a man-made storm. The thunder and lightning grips the audience as very real.

At the main gate to the amphitheater the girls asked for a drink. From the mountains in Wyoming I heard a crash of thunder.

"Let's get to the car and get ahead of the traffic rush, and then we can stop for a pop."

I was more concerned about the traffic than the thunder. It is eleven miles from Spearfish to Belle Fourche. That was eleven miles to travel in a hurry. The storm was much closer than we had thought. We got back on highway # 85 and sped north.

To the left we could see that the storm was no longer in Wyoming. It was close. There were lightning strikes all over the place to the West.

Berniece was very concerned. "Stop! Don't go any further! Turn around we have to go back!" There was pleading terror in her voice.

We could not stop or turn around on the busy narrow road. Besides, there was as much or more storm behind us than ahead so we traveled on.

In a lightning flash the girls spotted a funnel cloud.

Berniece was quite upset. From the twelve year old sprouts in the back seat came,

"But Grandma, we have never seen a twister before and it is so COOL."

Dirty Dishes

Wednesday 7.30 PM, and we were to be in Canada on Saturday. It was not pitch dark, but there was really no twilight left. We had just crossed the Red River in northern Texas. Coming to the curve in the road as it wound up the rise on the north side of the river there was a semi trailer parked on the shoulder of the highway. An approaching car had its lights on high beam. That made it hard to see. There was also a black narrow tar patch across the road or so it looked to me. I ran over it. Do you ever stop for a patch job on the pavement?

That wasn't a tar patch. It was an iron bar. It hit up under the Chev and made a ringing sound like a high toned bell. Next the shift lever on the steering column was fluttering like the wings on a migrating grass hopper. In a hundred yards of travel the buzzing stopped. I didn't stop. Let the Texas trucker load his own spilled scrap iron.

Liberal, Kansas was where we met the next stop light. When it turned green our Chev would not move. Moving the shift lever around let the car go backward. Shifting to drive and stepping on the gas did nothing. I, in a flustered frame of mind, moved the lever to first gear and raced the motor. We went through that red light like a jack rabbit that had gotten a hard boot in the rear.

Early the next morning I called S.G.I. (Saskatchewan Government Insurance)

"Good Morning, may I speak to the senior adjuster? Hello, Bill,, I just ran over a piece of iron on the road and knocked the transmission out of my car."

"It is too bad that you did not call before. The adjuster was at your place yesterday."

"Ya, but that wouldn't help, I am in Liberal, Kansas."

"Well, it may take us a week to get your car adjusted in Kansas."

"Please, Bill, we have to be home on Sunday at the latest." I nearly sobbed.

"Well, can you pay for it there and bring us the bills?" the chief adjuster of the Prince Albert branch suggested..

We drove to Garden City, Kansas. There the Chevrolet garage did not have a rebuilt transmission to fit our car. The nearest one would be at Dodge City, away to the east.

I felt pleased with myself. We were going to save our insurance company the price of an independent adjuster which may have doubled the cost of the repair. Maybe so we would have to skimp on meals the last of the way home.

The Chevy people installed a used transmission for us. It used up a day. I was not so smart after all. We had a U- drive car. It would have taken about two and a half hours to go and get the rebuilt part ourselves.

Ivan and Mary Muri, Berniece and I had been on a quick little trip to see our Texas cousins, Selma and Shorty Lutz. We crawled into the rental car that I had signed for and that meant that I had to drive. Compared to our old Chevrolet the instrument panel of the U-drive looked like the command post on space craft. It was past our usual meal time so we were hunting food. Every café we came to had some reason or other why we would not strop, mostly because I had driven past the entrance to the parking lot. Then I receive some navigation coaching.

"Slow down! There is a McDonalds and the lot is empty. Turn in right here."

I followed those instructions to a T. We were at the Golden Arches.

Inside looking at the menus board I saw the Big Happy Meal Deal for $1. Bill Redekopp's words came to me, 'Can you pay for the transmission yourself?' Here was the place to start economizing. A big meal for one dollar when the double burgers cost over two bucks.

To the girl behind the counter I said, "I'll have the big happy meal deal."

It seemed that she couldn't believe her ears, so I repeated my order. My three friends went for the same thing.

The poor girl with the cute little bonnet was having a terrible time to keep from smiling, but she said, "That will be four dollars please."

As I handed over the said amount of cash there were titters and giggles coming from the cooking department. There was not another person eating in the place so we had no trouble finding a table. Soon a young man brought our order. We each got a bun smaller than a hockey puck and a meat patty slightly bigger than a twenty five cent piece, and what's more, we each had a little cardboard house to put together.

It took Ivan about three minutes to get back to the order counter, "I guess we are not as young as we thought. Give us four Big Double Macs loaded." He had had enough of the kid's meal.

Out at the car Mary would see that we had a licence plate proclaiming this car was driven by a V.I.P.

We were home Sunday night.

On Tuesday, Chris Nelson, the insurance adjuster that regularly called at our shop took my statement and receipts. He called the bank to check on the US cash exchange rate and that was it.

In time, the cheque for the repair came. Adding twelve dollars to the cheque, we were able to trade with Clarence at his store for a dish washer.

Forty years earlier I had a new pair of riding boots. They were made to measure, fit like a glove and had white inserts in the tops. This was before the time of city people adopting cowboy boots. Mine had the leather underslung heels. They were big high hard heels that would jar your spine every step. There was no way that a foot would go through a stirrup with those boots. I was proud of my boots but they were killers to walk with or even stand in.

Well, with boots like that, it was natural to take a small riding job for a few days. Donald Burton and Arling Newton had this idea that they could buy a bunch of horses in the south west corner of Saskatchewan, trail them north and make a bunch of dollars selling these animals as bush horses to work in the lumber camps.

Talk about planning and preparations! Woodrow and I threw our saddles in the trunk of Arling's Plymouth, crawled into the back seat and we were off to find them horses. Albert Young at the community pasture west of Val Marie was the man to contact. We ate the evening meal with the cowboys, carpenters and the Youngs. There was a lot of building going on at Young's ranch yard.

After supper Albert Young and Arling went out to talk horses.

Donald, Woodrow and I were still in the cook house when Donald asked, " Mrs. Young, would you like some help with the dishes?"

"Oh, that would be heavenly. I have to do the payroll for all of the people that are working here at the pasture."

"Woodrow can wash and Bernie will be glad to dry them." With that he went to join in the horse talk.

It turned out to be a long drawn out job.

The next day the time was spent scouting for horses. We were back at Youngs for supper.

When the staff had gone out, Woodrow asked, "Mrs. Young, would you like some help with the dishes?"

"Yes, thank you Woodrow, that would be a big help ."

"Good, Bernie can wash and Donald can dry. I'm going to feed the pigs." And Woodrow grabbed the pail of kitchen scraps and was gone.

Donald called, "Come back."

Woodrow kept on the trail to the barn.

Donald went to the door, and he shouted, "Woodrow come back here."

Woodrow kept right on going.

Now that was a long evening. There were granite plates and cups from the noon meal and the big pressure cooker that had been taken out to the roundup crew. There had been eighteen at the table that evening, and that meant a lot of pots and pans, too.

Mrs. Young was a good cook and she did not spare the dishes and kettles.

Ever since that time I have been rather shy when it comes to doing dishes. That, too, is why I am glad that I ran over that crow bar in Texas, and we got a dishwasher.

That Rabbit

Our granddaughter Robyn was in grade two. She sent Grandma and I a letter telling us about her pet rabbit. Her dad bought the rabbit at a pet store. It has soft fur and it lives in a little house beside the garage she wrote.

Grandma and I joined the little girl in her glory of having a furry little friend.

We have a little grey bush rabbit that lives in our back yard. For the sake of discussion, we call our rabbit Benjy. We could not guarantee that it is the same rabbit we see every day. They all look the same and there could be many of them that hide in the bushes behind our house.

The first snowfall of the winter left four inches of soft white powdery snow on the ground. I took out my cross country skis. I carried them out the front gate and stepped on and pushed the lock down on each boot with my ski poles. I went out to the corner, turned and went past the church. Half a block up Victory Street, I went across a vacant lot to the back lane. There I turned towards home and through our side gate. At the corner of the house I took off the skis. I needed to give them a good waxing.

In the morning I found that the little cotton tails that live in our back yard had used only the left ski track, but it was used good. The other track was white with the ski groove still showing. It looked like dozens of bunnies had run up and down my track. I had to write to Robyn.

Dear Robyn:
  Yesterday I was out with my skis. I only went a half a block. My skis needed wax real bad, as they would hardly slide at all.

This morning when I took the garbage out to the pick up spot, I found that a rabbit had messed up my ski trail. I don't think that it was nice of that bunny to do such a thing. I don't ski on his trail so why would he run in my ski trail. I do not think that is very fair of the rabbit.

I like to be fair with the rabbits but this one sure is not fair with me. Imagine trying to ski when a rabbit has packed down one side of the trail. It is not right.

Before I signed off, there was a page of complaining about the rabbit.

I mailed my sob story to Robyn. Her answer was brief and to the point.

Dear Grandpa

You have a problem

        Love
        Robyn

Hit the Jackpot

The whole country side was glaring white. The snow was deep and the temperature was forty below Fahrenheit. The reflection of the sun on the snow was rather blinding at Leoville, Saskatoon , Regina and Minot, ND. By the time we were in Denver my eyes were sore, even thou there was no snow there. Back on the plane I had a window seat. I strained my eyes for the whole four hour flight to Houston, Texas.

The air terminal at Hobby Field was dim and shadowy.

At a pay phone I was going to call cousin Shorty to let them know when they might expect Berniece and I to arrive. I still had a touch of snow blindness from the north. My glasses were in the suitcase that Berniece was waiting for or guarding in the baggage entrance. I tried to call Shorty. My call did not go through, and the phone box kept my quarter. The next call did not work, neither did the quarter which Texas Bell glomed onto. It seemed like a quarter of a mile walk to Travelers Aid. All they had were four quarters that I traded a dollar bill for. Hurry! Getting the call to Shorty was uppermost in my mind. Then beside the call thought was the nagging wonder of how Berniece was doing. Did she have the suitcases, or was she lost along with the luggage, or had she been kidnapped. Oh that was a long walk. Why were we not back at the ranch feeding cows?

Back to the phone in the dark hallway. One more failure, one more twenty-five cent piece gone over the hill.

I was confused, lost and bewildered. I held out my palm with three coins left. Two dark lads approached. The taller light chocolate complected fellow picked one of my US quarters out of my hand, as smooth as a hen picks a kernel of grain. He inserted it in the next pay phone and started to talk. His buddy was short, and with a round ebony black face that showed the whitest set of teeth when he smiled.

I was exasperated. The phone, the location, the black man that took my quarter, everything was against me. I pressed the coin return on the phone and again got nothing. I was getting huffy. I slapped the side of the phone that had my money. Suddenly the coin return freed up. The slot was overloaded, I scooped out coins as fast as I could and they still kept coming. I had a hand full and the more I tried to hold, the more I spilled. My new found black friend was dancing and shouting, "You Won Man, You Won that Spin, You Won Man." He was on his knees gathering up stray quarters that he then poured into my jacket pocket. I had the phone return cleaned out and still had a heaping handful of coins. The chocolate faced guy finished his call, got the quarter returned, and dropped it into my hand. Out of my hand splashed more money that fell to the floor. Little Ebony was back on his knees gathering up my silver. He shoved that into my pocket like he did the first handful and went on his way.

    I said to myself, 'I like those guys.' Then I called Shorty.

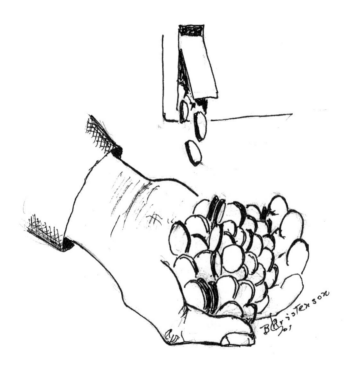

Tornado

It was a big old car! Orville and I stood beside the Buick. To Jack Wilson, a retired post master from Wisconsin, it was not just a Buick. It was a 1962 Buick Electra 225 coupe. It must have been the longest car that General Motors had ever built. From the rear edge of the door to the tail light was much more than the arm span of a very big man.

"I wish you would buy the monster and drive it back to Canada." That was Orville's faint wish.

"Do you think he would sell it to me?"

"Well, he should. He is in his eighty's now and is not capable of driving it anymore."

A plan clicked right away.

Our flight from Saskatoon, Saskatchewan to Houston, Texas, had been different. The landing in Regina was so rough that the wings of the Boeing 747 flopped around too much to suit me. At Minot, N.D. it was even rougher. There we sat in the airport terminal for eleven hours while they flew a mechanic and thirty-five gallons of brake fluid in from Denver. We wandered around and watched the Saskatchewan type blizzard bring visibility down to zero. At sundown the storm let up somewhat. The airline mechanics had a large tarp draped over the wing of the airplane. A tiger torch was giving all of the heat that it could. By watching the mechanics from our vantage point inside of the terminal, we figured that the heat from the torch did not amount to a row of beans. We on flight 387 got two complementary meals from the airline.

Nine forty-five, and we were in the air to Denver. The red headed flight attendant was pushy. She had one hundred and six meals to push into twenty-eight passengers. The rest of the 387 people had found other travel plans. In Denver we were given vouchers for dinner, hotel room and breakfast. To sleep at 2:30 AM. and breakfast at five o'clock, made for a short night.

From Denver to Houston I had a window seat. If it would not have been for the glass, I might have had my head out past the tip of the wing. I had to see it all.

The area where the telephones were in Houston was dimly lit. I was trying to call Shorty (Orville). I ran out of quarters.

Because of two young black men, I got my call through to Shorty. Those boys were very helpful.

Oh, yes, the plan for the Buick! 'If Jack would sell me the old car cheap, we could drive to the airport at Houston, and the first black boy we would see before we boarded the plane, I'd just hand him the keys to the Buick.

There were two reasons that dumb plan would not work. In Texas it takes about a month to clear a title for an automobile. The other one was Jack.

"Will you sell me your car?" I asked.

With a horrified look Jack answered, "Oh, no, that would be like cutting off my arms. That car has been a family member for some years now. I will never let it go."

On the road back to Shorty's, he explained further why he did not appreciate the Buick.

I must add, a person that has not lived through a tornado, will have a different attitude than a person that has been through one or more.

"We got the tornado warning about five that evening. They called it a class three, and it could be upgraded to four or five by the time it got to us. The eye of the storm was between Eagle Pass and Laredo. Now that is just a hundred and some miles from us. The storm was predicted to follow a path along the Rio Grand. The river is only ten miles south of our place."

"We had done this before. We packed our things that we would not leave in the storm path. We called Jack and Mary. When they heard that we had to outrun a tornado, they didn't know what we were talking about. Get your most valued possessions in your car right away. We will come by your place and travel with you."

"When we got there, they had two pillows, the teapot from her fine china set, (no cups but the teapot) and Jack's comb and brush and electric razor. That was all they wanted to take along."

Imagine a comb and brush, and he is bald.

It was dark by the time we got to Falfurrais, where we turned west. I was in the lead with our Ford pickup, then Jack, and finally Selma with our Dodge coupe. There was no traffic coming, but in the high wind and dust it was hard to see the road. My idea was to go west and then northwest and we would get behind the storm. Well, here come Selma driving like a mad woman. Jack was sitting in their car ten miles down the road with a flat tire. We went back to help. There was nothing in the trunk of the Buick but the spare tire, jack and wheel wrench. I changed the tire and threw in the flat, wheel disc and fender skirt and slammed the lid.

There was Jack fumbling for his keys. The wind was so strong that a person could hardly stand up. He opened his trunk. If the car was not facing the wind, his trunk lid would have been blown away. He got out the big chrome wheel cover, knelt down to put it on. I slapped it on and shouted, 'Come on Jack we are driving away from the eye of the storm to save our lives.'

Jack was disappointed in me rushing him when he said, "Shorty, I never drive my Buick without the hub caps and fender skirts on."

More Jackpot

Friday morning I went to get the Los Angeles Times. There was the paper machine right across the drive way from our motel door. It did not give me the daily paper, or my money back. Saturday morning was a repeat of the day before.

Jim and Maggie Mumm were at an Organic Producers convention. Berniece and I were there to be exploring partners with our grandchildren. Lisa was ready for her tenth birthday, and Alex was six. The six of us shared a suite in a motel across the street from Disneyland. On Saturday evening to kick our shoes off and relax, we watched a movie on TV.

The picture was not one of the big box office specials. It was low comedy. The poor garage mechanic who had been a boxer was trying to live down his past. Big Louie wanted the ex-fighter to get back in the boxing ring, so they could rig fights and clean up a fortune. The hero's girl friend did not want that. Big Louie had a group of aids all dressed in black, pin striped suits. With these fellows, Big Louie ran every racket there was in town. They were forever grabbing their baseball bats and rushing with the big black limmo to do some of Big Louie's business. It was very laughable. The show, with pop and pizza, was more or less a last party for Berniece and I. We were going home on Sunday morning. It was late to bed on Saturday night, but it had been fun.

Sunday morning, I again tried for the Los Angeles Times. Not like the week day issue that cost fifty cents, Sunday's paper was one dollar and fifty cents. I put six quarters into the machine but the door was still locked solid. The coin return would not work. It now had two dollars and fifty cents of mine. I curiously put a finger up into the coin return and felt a bit of paper. I pulled out a candy bar wrapper and it was followed by thirty-seven twenty-five cent pieces. I got the paper and went back to our lodgings. I showed the hand full of coins.

Alex was so compassionate.

"Grandpa, that might be one of Big Louie's capers, and he will miss that money, but when he comes, I can tell him that you have gone to Canada."

Another Jackpot

Woodrow Newton picked me up with his Dad's car. Our destination was the Friday night dance in Hodgeville, Saskatchewan. It was in the early spring. The dirt roads were muddy in places. A mile west of town there was a set of muddy ruts in the center of the road. Woodrow stopped to let an oncoming car use the ruts first. Everything looked good until the last few feet. Then the approaching car jumped out of the ruts and careened off Uncle Ben's Black Plymouth.

The other car was a Chevrolet. Its passenger who was slightly tippsy said that he would pay for all damages.

The hall was full, the girls were pretty and the music had a romantic melody. It was a great night.

We were on our way home. Woodrow negotiated the muddy ruts without a problem.

Then he said, "I might be in the Jackpot when Dad gets home."

"Where is he?

"Yesterday morning I took him to the train with the old Ford truck. He is at a Stock Grower's convention and won't be home until Tuesday." A further thought, "When he sees this smashed up fender he may blow a fuse.The last thing he said to Mom was, DON'T LET WOODROW DRIVE MY CAR."

Bedtime Story

Berniece and I had our two youngest grandsons on a holiday trip to South Dakota's Black Hills. Our trail led out of Saskatchewan, into Montana, across the corner of Wyoming and finally to South Dakota.

At Belle Fourche nearly in the shadow of the Black Hills, we registered in at our favorite motel. A room with two double beds and a television set. That was all of our needs wrapped up real easy.

Our young traveling companions had napped occasionally in the back seat. Now at bed time they were brimming with life.

Grandma announced, "Boys, it is time for bed. Get into your pajamas now."

Each boy took his turn in the bathroom where he changed into his PJ's. He came out, folded his clothes and laid them neatly away for the next day.

Riley was six years old. "My dad used to read me a bedtime story and then Mom sings me a lullaby."

Cole was ten. "My mom or dad used to read me a story but now I make one up before I go to sleep."

Riley was not one to let tradition fade away.

"Grandpa, we need a story."

"Well, all right. Get the covers up to your chins and lie still and listen."

"This story is about dinosaurs," I told them.

Minicryptugoreus.

Why are Minicryptugoreus so hard to see? Why do children some times see them and their parents are never able to see them? Big people do not know where to look for Minicryptugoreus. Kids sometimes see them where men with the big yellow trucks have made black patches on the hi-way.

Minicryptugoreus are the smallest of all the dinosaur family. They are the blackest of all of the dinosaurs. They used to be the friendliest of all dinosaurs, but now they are only friendly to children. They never let big people see them.

One day Noogl Scook Minicryptugoreus was napping on a black spot on the hi-way. The sun was warm and the clouds were white, and Noogl fell asleep.

It was too bad that Mr. Grumpstump had a flat tire close to that black spot on the hi-way. He had to leave his car and walk for help. When he saw Noogl sleeping he took his foot and kicked the poor little dinosaur . It hurt and Noogl did not think that it was a nice thing for Mr. Grumpstump to do. Then he saw Mr. Grumpstump kick a pretty flower. Now that was mean.

Noogl found another black spot to nap on.
There Mr. Stembump stepped on Noogl's tail. He had to go out of his way to do it, too.

Mr. Stembump had been walking on the other side of the road where he stepped in some mud. Mr. Stembump left muddy tracks across the road and there was even mud on Noogl's tail where it had been stepped on.

Prince Noogl Scook Minicryptugoreus went home. Noogl wondered why people had to be so mean.

That evening Queen Minicryptugoreus had a marshmallow roast for Noogl and all of his little friends. While they were setting around the camp fire, Noogl told of his misadventure of the morning. All of the guests at the marshmallow roast were dumbfounded to hear of what had happened to their friend. After a long talk about the situation, they decided that no big person would ever see a Minicryptugoreus. They also planned to hide on black spots on the hi-way.

ZZZZZZZ

Riley sat up in bed. "Aw ,Grandpas' fallen asleep,"

"If we can get the book without waking Grandpa, I'll read the rest of the story," Cole offered.

Like two elves the urchins crept out of bed, and as robbers in the night relieved Grandpa of the book. Sitting on the edge of the bed, Cole took up the story.

If they ever saw Mr. Grumpstump or Mr. Stembump they would tell them to be kind to dinosaurs and animals and little people and even flowers.

That is why big people just don't see Minicryptugoreus any more. One time while riding with their Dad in the blue van, Robyn and Eric were certain that they saw a Minicryptugoreus.

"Too bad that Grandpa fell asleep. He won't know how the story ends," Cole observed.

"Grandma, Mom always sings me a lullaby when I go to sleep," Riley reminded.

"Get under the covers again, both of you and I'll sing a little bit."

With a voice that had been heard in many choirs, Grandma sang:

> Little papoose in your cradle high
> Swung up in the dancing tree
> Looking up at the starry sky
> Tell me what do you see
>
> Shining moon with his face so bright
> Watching with care so mild
> So go to sleep and sleep this night
> Sleep little Indian child.

"Good Night, boys."

"Good Night, Grandma."

"Grandpa, it is time to quit that fake snore and faint grin, and come to bed."

The Bird Bath

Berniece pointed out the green set of kettles on the store shelf.

"Oh boy, they look good and they are so cheap." I was all hept up to buy them right then and there.

"They are of a thin material and maybe they have not much for quality either," she said.

I was still super enthused, "At that price we can't go wrong."

"We don't really need them." She had second thoughts.

"Just feel this frying pan. It is so light and easy to lift compared to the old cast iron ones that we have. And, besides, they have a nice finish. This green is so outstanding compared with what we have." Then I thought of the clincher. "I heard that cooking in aluminum pots could give a person the start of Alzheimer disease."

In spite of all of the good advice, I bought the set of green kettles.

After a few months at home the green paint chipped off in spots. The bottoms warped from the heat of the stove. If you put food in them to cook, it burnt.

You may think that I would never go back to that store again. Well, I cannot remember where we, I mean, where I bought them. It was my own fault. I should have listened to my wife.

For years the green pots got cussed and abused by me. Berniece never used them. The light handy frying pan was sometimes used for poaching eggs. It was tough to clean up even after a job like that.

The green pan was in the middle of a nest of pans. When ever you needed a cast iron pan, there was the old green one in the way. Just like a mongrel dog in the corral gate when you are trying to get cows brought in.

Berniece has taken a liking to birds among her flowers. I built her a bird feeder. The birds don't come near it but the bird seed that got spilled has started to grow. If we had a goat it could be a goat feeder. She tried a bird bath on the ground after a collection of birds were drinking in the puddle where I left the garden hose running too long.

I said, "I will build you a bird bath in the tree close to the window. There we can sit and watch with the binoculars and have a real close up view of the birds."

It was not much of a job to screw a platform onto the tree where it had a stub of a cut off branch sticking out on the right side and at the right angle. I set the green frying pan on the shelf on the tree. With an inch or two of water in it that should be ideal.

What a sight! The green pan surrounded by lighter green leaves. Now the neighbours white tom cat has climbed the tree and is sitting beside the bird bath.

What a picture. A white cat beside a green frying pan up in a green tree.

My First Sheep

I was twelve years old that beautiful evening in June. Uncle Sidney had come to sheer our sheep.

Every thing was ready for the sheering. The sheep had been in the lean-to section of the barn since noon. That was so they would be warm, and sweat into the wool close to their bodies. It made shearing much easier, than if they were cold. There were a couple of chunks of old canvas laid near the barn door. This was there for Uncle to set the sheep on to shear them. There was a board to set his oilstone on for sharpening his sheer. A pail of water with disinfectant in it to dip the shears in every so often was the total of the preparation. This was on the west side of the barn. There was a hay rack parked on the south side, with its pole at the far corner of the building. At the back end of the hay rack were the remains of a good rain we had the day before. This mud puddle was about four inches deep. Being so close to the barn the water did have a slight amber tint.

Uncle Sidney had his first sheep sitting up on end , and had the wool rolling down in soft yellow folds. I had watched sheep being sheered for most of my years. I had seen it so many times that I knew how it should be done. Uncle was on his second sheep. Why shouldn't I pitch in and help. I asked to have a sheep to shear. That generous offer was turned down. I asked in a different manner. That too was refused. The third sheep was near finished.

"Well, why can't I have a sheep to do?" I begged.

"All right, you can take that old ewe that has no wool on her belly, or one side."

"No, don't let that kid shear, he will only mess things up for us," Uncle Albin had a negative notion.

"Oh, he might as well try it. Then he might stop pestering us," reasoned Uncle Sidney. He added, "Catch the old sheep and sit her up on the grass. When you are ready, I'll hand you the clipper."

The sheep was in position, and I was on the threshold of a great career. I would grow up to be a sheep shearer. "Gemme the shears."

What a struggle! The wool did not open up to my effort like it did for my uncle. With many snips, like I was cutting paper in grade one, I got a start. The leather hand strap was too big for my hand. It was more of a hindrance than a help. It would be the height of humiliation to ask to have it removed. Only in some European countries the women sheared without a hand strap guard.

Now that I had a start, the wool was rolling down over the side of the old girl. It was not creamy gold in color, but more of a dusty grey. It was sure coming good. Maybe I nicked the sheep with the shear. Whatever the cause, she started to struggle. I was losing control. I lost my balance. The sheep gained her footing, with all four feet on the ground. Somehow I had gotten my arms around the animals neck, but was lying with my body on her back. At the start of the tussle, the shear had opened up. I pinched it closed, but the trouble was that the blades were not together but back to back. This left two eight inch sword like blades exposed and reflecting the sunlight. The sheep with those spindly little legs took off, with me as extra baggage on her back. Her escape route was clouded by the wool that I had sheared, covering her face. She was seeing too well, so we went past the corner of the barn and over the big old pig resting in the mud puddle. In the scramble the pig got her head between the spokes of the wagon wheel. The pig would not back up, but just squealed to hi-heaven. Oh what a noise! The frail little old sheep would not back up either. She had her mind made up to take me right on over the pig. She made a dozen little jumps to get going. Each thrust banged my shoulder into the wooden beam of the hay rack that we were fighting under. The old pig that had been so rudely disturbed in her sow sauna was complaining, with ear splitting sounds of protest.

Uncle Sidney had finished his sheep. He and Uncle Albin were able to calm their laughter enough to pull the sheep and me from on top of the pig. We cleared the water all of the way through our discord. With us out of the way, the pig got her head out of the wagon wheel. With a couple of grunty snorts, she became scarce. The sheep was returned to the sweat pen, and I stood with blood dripping on the grass. When the shear was open and being waved around, I sliced two times at my left thumb.

Oliver Moe drove up to our big project at that time. He was driving the Ford bug. This was a California built race car that Uncle Sidney had bought ten years earlier. Uncle Dave was using it while he farmed at Kelstern.

"Dave is bringing a pair of horses back form over east. He would like Bernie to meet him and bring them home."

As I was no longer needed at the shearing job, I was sent to the house for a bandage on my thumb. The cuts were not bad, but they left two scars. Beside my thumb nail I had white marks just like the brand of the old 77 ranch. With a clean white cotton bandage on my left hand, I was soon in the navigator's seat in the bug.

We met Uncle David north west of Hodgeville. He was riding bare-back. With a,"Glad to see you." I was boosted to the back of one of the horses, and I was riding home.

The ego crushing deal with the old crock of a sheep was still remembered. With the rhythm of the horse and the white stars above, what could be better? My thumb smarted and my shoulder ached. It would be much better to become a cowboy, than a sheep shearer.

Love a Horse

It was an honor when my niece Linda asked me to give the toast to the bride at her wedding. She and Howie Wall made their home at Hodgeville for a while. In time they had two daughters and a son and lived at Luseland, Saskatchewan.

Three summers in a row Howie , Linda and the kids would bring their van and holiday trailer and camp in our yard.

Layne was a pre-schooler. He had total freedom of the yard. Our collie dog, Rowdy, was so glad to find a new friend that could spend the live long day playing. It was not all frivolous play. If they found one white hen in the garden, it was a Cowboy and Indian type race. The hen always saved her feathers by running for dear life for the chicken pen, and flying over the fence to safety. The only thing more exciting for this pair of buddies was two hens in the garden. They would chase the first hen back to the pen and the other dumb cluck would scratch around as if her little white body had been missed in the roundup. As soon as the garden guards could get back, then she was the object of the next run.

While Layne and Rowdy were hunting and exploring, the girls Holly and Tricia were in the big round corral with Hicky, the grey saddle mare. The grass was high enough in the corrals to feed a horse for three weeks. The gate to the corral that had water running through was opened and closed many times during the day, and Hicky, never went thirsty.

The second summer was a copy of the first. Layne and Rowdy and the hens. Holly and Tricia and Hicky. The difference was that the girls would get the horse close in beside the corral rails. One girl stood at the horse's shoulder and patted with feminine little hands while the other climbed the rails and crawled on the horse. What a thrill to be on a horse even if she just stood still. A couple of days of that and then one girl led Hicky by holding a few hairs of the horse's mane, while her sister did the riding.

Summer number three and the girls were older. Hicky got to wear a bridle. When Holly stood in front of the horse, the grey nag would open her mouth and accept the bit, then lower her head so the bridle could be slipped over her ears. Whenever I slapped a saddle on that horse, it was next to roughhouse tactics to put a bridle on her.

The corral gates were all opened and they had the run of the calving pasture. This was a thirty acre fenced plot with tiny clumps of spruce, aspen and willow and with a small stream of water flowing through. It was a struggle for the girls to get Hicky to cross where the stream was narrow and hard ground on each side, but as they circled back to the corral, she would willingly wade across a long swampy part of the steam. Hicky had what was called, a bad case of Barn Sour. That meant that she was only comfortable at the barn. She wanted to always stay in the corral and be petted.

That was the last summer that we lived on Spruce Creek Ranch. Katherine, who knew Hicky, before we bought her, had asked for the first chance to buy the horse. That is where Hicky went.

It must have been in summer number two that Howie, Linda and family were transferred to Kerrobert, Saskatchewan.

After the last summer with Hicky, Holly bicycled out to a chuck wagon racer's stable.

"I like horses. Could I have a job here?" Holly was straight forward.

"No, there is no place for a girl around here. Girls aren't strong enough to do this kind of work." Wayne Schlossier was painfully straight forward, too. "I have to go now."

"Can I look at your horses?" Holly asked.

"Yes, but don't go in the corral," and he was gone.

Holly looked around and found a fork, shovel, broom and a wheel barrow and four horse stalls that were in dire need of cleaning. Three hours later the stable was spotless, with a refuse pile out beside the corral. Holly was undaunted while she peddled back to town. In a day or two she was back visiting with the chuck wagon horses.

"By gosh, kid, did you clean my barn the other day?" Wayne sort of growled.

"It sure needed cleaning, so I did it."

"Pretty good for a slip of a girl," was his begrudging compliment.

"Well, I like horses and they should have things nice, too," Holly countered.

"I have a bunch of horses over in another pasture that I have to feed. Want to come along?"

"Sure."

That was the beginning of a friendship that lasted to his last day. Holly was in her glory riding and caring for horses.

One bay mare was Holly's favorite. She and Dennis were about to be married. He went to buy the bay mare from Wayne as a wedding present for Holly.

"Well, a fella in Calgary wants that horse. He offered twenty-eight hundred dollars for her," that was Wayne's first thought.

"Holly sure likes that horse," was all Dennis could answer.

"Aw shucks, for Holly the price should be half. Give me fourteen hundred."

The young groom to be must have swallowed hard at that figure.

"I think I will cut the price in half again. Give me seven hundred and I will have the mare's registration papers sent in and changed to Holly Murphy as the owner," Wayne offered.

Berniece and I were a little bit early for Holly and Dennis's wedding. We did not know where the church was but we did find it. Early is better than late, so we went in. Layne was one of the ushers. He led us to the very front row and seated us in a short pew that had one person sitting there. This man was tall and thin, and his face had fine lines or tiny wrinkles. The wrinkles were not outstanding like his clear eyes. His hands were sun baked brown and sinewy. His looks went well with his fine tailored western style grey suit. The high crowned wide brimmed hat that was on the pew beside him, gave the finishing touch to the look of this old time horseman.

There were the two ushers and the three of us in the church.

The gentleman that just had to be Wayne Schlossier looked at us and asked, "Why the hell am I here, and why are you here, too?"

I answered him, "Oh, I guess we are all here, because we love a girl that loves horses."

The Ford Coupe

I had owned the 1929 Ford Coupe for exactly forty years. When I got it, it was basically all there. It ran very nice after my brother- in law, Norman Woods, rebuilt the engine. It was stored at the Woods' farm. We lived in Lethbridge, Alberta but never did get the Ford coupe to Alberta.

One summer our nieces and their Mom and Dad and brother were here from the States for a holiday. We went to the Woods farm and started the Model A. I took Elizabeth and Sylvia for a ride in the old car. It was a down hill curve to the main road. I got up a fair bit of speed going to the road. I had no license and when the Mounted Police whizzed past Norman's driveway, I found that I had no brakes either. The cops were in a hurry, they did not even see us.

This car was bought new by a storekeeper at Success, Saskatchewan.

Mr. Frank Jackson had a reliable Dodge truck. He organized a cream route. That meant that on Monday, Wednesday and Friday he would make a trip around the countryside and pick up full cream cans and deliver them to the creamery in Swift Current. The following day he would back track his route and leave the empty cream cans. For his overnight stay in the city he would be at the Imperial Hotel at the corner of Central Ave. and Railway Street.

One summer evening in 1941, during world war two, Frank met a sad man. Gasoline was rationed and tires impossible to get unless you would qualify for a permit from the War Time Prices and Control Board. It was the storekeeper that had the Ford coupe. He sat in a chair in the hotel lobby with a woebegone look. Frank sat down beside him.

"It is such a short distance from home to the city, and I blew out five tires on the trip in today, and the tires cannot be repaired. New ones for me are out of the question. The Wartime

Prices and Trade Board will not let merchants buy tires," the Ford owner complained.

Before the evening was over Mr. Jackson had bought the car. New cars were also not to be bought.

On the empty can run, Frank stopped to see Cliff Jones.

"Say, Cliff, how are the tires on your car?"

"Three are nearly new and one and the spare are between fair and poor," Cliff answered.

"I have a car in Swift Current for you, but it has no tires. Take two of your good tires and come with me in the morning. When we get to the city, you can go to the War Time Price and Control Board and get two new tires."

That was the way it worked, and Cliff was driving the sporty blue Ford Coupe.

One fall I drove a grain truck for Newton's harvest outfit. While we were working at Cliff Jones's farm, he and I got to be good friends. Ten years later I stopped to say hello to Cliff. He was harvesting oats right along the road. He stopped his machine and we stood in the stubble field and visited. He looked at my new red and white station wagon with the Alberta licence plates.

"You can't take that car into the mountains for a fishing trip." Mr. Jones more or less laid down the law. "You need my old Ford coupe."

That was when I became the owner of the Ford that I never did get time to take fishing in the mountains. I had every intention of restoring the old car to new car condition. Every decade it seemed to deteriorate more. Then the cost of the restoration climbed like mad. The next road block to its restoration was my health. I could not do the job myself.

Berniece and I had done up a book that no publisher was too interested in.

With a family conference with the Ford coupe as the subject, we came to the conclusion that no one had the time to fix up Cliff's old car. The last word was, "Sell the car and publish your book. After you're gone it will be easier for us to divide up a pile of books than the Ford coupe." I sold the Ford.

Rabbits Don't Wear Diamonds

In 1932, what we now call the western world, was in a sad state. Why it was that way has many theories. Frank said that it was due to greed and gaiety of the twenties. Our economy was not strong enough to stand the spendthrifts sucking money out one end and greedy guys taking more than their share out the other end. It just stretched our economy until it busted in the middle.

Factories closed, and mills ran at less than half their normal output. No one could afford to buy our grain or beef so nobody here had any money.

Mr. Frank Burton was a director of the Vanguard Hospital board. This two story red brick building was a matter of life and death to the people of a very wide area.

Frank was a community leader. He had a brown mustache and a commanding voice. After a board meeting that was not cheerful at all, he stopped in at the pool hall.

To some lounger, Frank mentioned, "I don't see how we can keep the hospital open. The whole staff are going with hardly any pay"

This remark started a brainstorming session. Many ideas were thought of and discarded.

"Those ideas won't work because they all take local money. There is no local money."

"How can we get outside money to support the hospital? If we could shoot a thousand rabbits and sell the fur, we would have some cash. It would cost a fortune for the shells to shoot a thousand rabbits."

Frank, again the leader, "Over at my gravel pit there are straight banks on two sides. We could fence off the rest of the area. All we have to do is find enough chicken wire to close in the west and north sides and when we get the rabbits in, we would have them in the palm of our hand."

"How do we get the rabbits in this pen?"

Frank again, "We will spread the word far and wide that we are having a rabbit drive. If men are close enough together that a rabbit would not run back between them, we would herd them like sheep. The rabbits will run into the coulee at the Turkey Track Ranch, and that will lead them right to our trap. Those that come down past the Reed Ranch will hit the creek and we will bring them east. The ones from the hills northeast and the south will get to the creek and they will have to come west. The whole country is crawling with rabbits so we will get very many."

The fence was built. There was a very wide opening left for a gate. The plan was for twenty men to grab the wire and close the gate when the pen was full.

Our neighbors went rabbit driving. It was an eighteen mile trip for our local rabbits to get to the pen. One person would take a team of horses and a sleigh and have a whole gang with him. These guys would walk a while to scare out rabbits, then ride on the sleigh for a rest.

The long legged Jack Rabbits with the black ear tips were hopping along heading towards Frank's gravel pit. At the outer fringe of the great circle the men were not that close together. The people on the east side of the ring would live thirty miles from those on the west side. This was a large undertaking.

Some folks even took the family dog along. After many fruitless rabbit chases, some dogs took more interest in field mouse tracks, and others just gave up and trotted back home.

In the late afternoon rabbits poured out of the coulees onto the flat land west of the gravel pit. Soon they were joined by those in the creek, from east and west. At this stage of the game, men were within arms length of one another. As the rabbits moved closer to the open gate, the circle grew smaller. Soon men were shoulder to shoulder. The rabbits were caught. What a success!

Everyone wore a smile, and they were tired but the job was done.

One brave buck rabbit thought he saw a weak spot in the fence. It was not weak, but he charged it anyway. A section of the fence went down. More rabbits charged out. Men could not get to that spot fast enough to stop the stampede. In just more than a blink of the eye, the estimated six thousand rabbits were on the other side of the hill.

It was sundown of a hard day.

Frank's speech was heard by every one.

"It's OK boys. Them rabbits weren't wearing diamonds anyway."